CAAT
Success Handbook

A Simple, No-Nonsense Guide to the Canadian Adult Achievement Test

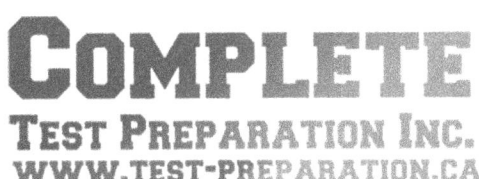

COMPLETE
Test Preparation Inc.
WWW.TEST-PREPARATION.CA

Copyright 2012 Complete Test Preparation Inc. All Rights Reserved.

Intellectual Property Rights This publication is protected by copyright. No part of this book may be reproduced, copied, distributed, or transmitted in any form or by any means—including graphic, electronic, or mechanical methods such as photocopying, recording, or information storage and retrieval systems—without the prior written permission of the publisher, except in the case of brief quotations embodied in critical reviews and certain other noncommercial uses permitted by copyright law.

Disclaimer & Limitation of Liability While the publisher and author have used their best efforts in preparing this book, they make no representations or warranties with respect to the accuracy or completeness of the contents. The advice and strategies contained herein may not be suitable for your situation. Test content and administration rules change frequently; readers are advised to verify all information with the official test providers. Complete Test Preparation Inc. shall not be liable for any loss of profit or any other commercial damages, including but not limited to special, incidental, consequential, or other damages.

Non-Affiliation Notice Complete Test Preparation Inc. is an independent publisher and is not affiliated with, endorsed by, or sponsored by any testing organization, educational institution, or government agency mentioned in this publication. All trademarks, service marks, and trade names are the property of their respective owners and are used for reference and identification purposes only.

We strongly recommend that students check with exam providers for up-to-date information regarding test content.

Complete Test Preparation Inc. is not affiliated with the makers of the CAAT, Creative Organizational Design (COD), who are not involved in the production of, and do not endorse this publication.
ISBN-13: 9781772451788

Version 10 March 2026

About Complete Test Preparation Inc.

Why Choose Complete Test Preparation? You want to spend your valuable study time where it counts the most. We've got you covered.

Since 2005, we have helped hundreds of thousands of students succeed with over 145 study guides and online courses. We know that tests change, which is why we keep our content current and relevant.

Study with a Purpose With this purchase, you are doing more than just preparing for a test. You are supporting a mission to improve education globally. We are proud to support charities that bring learning opportunities to those who need them most.

Learn more about our mission:
https://www.test-preparation.ca/charities-and-non-profits/

You have definitely come to the right place.
If you want to spend your valuable study time where it will help you the most - we've got you covered today and tomorrow.

Thank you for studying with us!

Published by
Complete Test Preparation Inc.
Victoria BC Canada

Visit us on the web at https://www.test-preparation.ca

Feedback

We welcome your feedback. Email us at feedback@test-preparation.ca with your comments and suggestions. We carefully review all suggestions and often incorporate reader suggestions into upcoming versions. As a Print on Demand Publisher, we update our products frequently.

CONTENTS

6   **The Road Map: Setting Your Pace**
       How this study guide is organized   7
       The 3-Week "Success Without Stress" Plan   8
       Getting the Most from Practice Questions   12
       After Completing a Practice Test   13

14   **Reading Between the Lines: Mastering the Message**
       Self-Assessment   18
       Answer Key   27
       Help with Reading Comprehension   30
       Reading Comprehension Strategy   31
       Drawing Inferences And Conclusions   38

43   **The Toolbox: Everyday Math for the Exam**
       Self-Assessment   47
       Answer Key   56
       Basic math Video Tutorials   60
       Fraction Tips, Tricks and Short-cuts   60
       Most Common Fraction Mistakes on a Test   66
       Decimal Tips, Tricks and Shortcuts   67
       Converting Decimals to Fractions   67
       Percent Tips, Tricks and Short-cuts   68
       How to Answer Basic Math Multiple Choice   70
       Order Of Operation   73

75   **Word Power: Unlocking the Big Ideas**
       Self-Assessment   79
       Answer Key   82
       Taming the Big Words: A Practical Guide   83

85   **Putting it all Together - Practice Test 1**
       Answer Key   125

140   **Rounding the Final Corner Practice Test 2**
       Answer Key   176

189   Cracking the Code How to Build your Vocabulary

Meaning in Context	192
Top 100 Common Vocabulary	207
Stem Words	211
Stem Words Practice Questions	222
Answer Key – Part I	228
Stem Words Practice Part II	231
Answer Key Part II	237
Most Common Prefix	240
Prefix Questions	243
Most Common Synonyms	251
Synonym Practice Questions	256
Most Common Antonyms	266
Antonym Practice Questions	271

280   Your Game Day Strategy: Calm, Cool, and Collected

Wrestling the "Test Anxiety" Monster	281

285   Online Resources

https://www.youtube.com/user/MrTestPreparation

The Road Map: Setting Your Pace

CONGRATULATIONS! By deciding to take the Canadian Adult Education Test (CAAT), you have taken the first step toward a great future! Of course, there is no point in taking this important examination unless you intend to do your best to earn the highest grade you possibly can. That means getting yourself organized and discovering the best approaches, methods and strategies to master the material. Yes, that will require real effort and dedication, but if you are willing to focus your energy and devote the study time necessary, before you know it you will be opening that letter of acceptance to the school of your dreams.

We know that taking on a new endeavour can be scary, and it is easy to feel unsure of where to begin. That's where we come in. This study guide is designed to help you improve your test-taking skills, show you a few tricks of the trade and increase both your competency and confidence.

The Canadian Adult Education Test

The CAAT exam has sections, vocabulary, number operations, problem solving and reading comprehension.

While we seek to make our guide as comprehensive as possible, note that like all exams, the CAAT might be adjusted at some future point. New material might be added, or content that is no longer relevant or applicable might be removed. It is always a good idea to give the materials you receive when you register to take the CAAT a careful review.

How this study guide is organized

This study guide is divided into four sections. The first section, self-assessments, which will help you recognize your areas of strength and weaknesses. This will be a boon when it comes to managing your study time most efficiently; there is not much point of focusing on material you have already got firmly under control. Instead, taking the self-assessments will show you where that time could be much better spent. In this area you will begin with a few questions to evaluate quickly your understanding of material that is likely to appear on the CAAT. If you do poorly in certain areas, simply work carefully through those sections in the tutorials and then try the self-assessment again.

The second section, tutorials, offers information in each of the content areas, as well as strategies to help you master that material. The tutorials are not intended to be a complete course, but cover general principles. If you find that you do not understand the tutorials, it is recommended that you seek out additional instruction.

Third, we offer two sets of practice test questions, similar to those on the CAAT Exam.

The 3-Week CAAT "Success Without Stress" Plan

Week 1: Foundations & The "Rules of the Road"
Focus: Re-learning how to take a test and mastering the basics of math and words.

- **Day 1: The Diagnostic "No-Pressure" Run**
  - Take a practice test with no timer. Circle anything that makes you scratch your head. This isn't about the score; it's about finding the gaps.
- **Day 2: Vocabulary — The Building Blocks**
  - Focus on **Synonyms and Antonyms**. I always tell students: look at the "charge" of the word (is it a positive or negative word?).
  - *Activity:* Start a "Pocket Glossary" of 10 new words today.
- **Day 3: Math — Back to Basics**
  - Review **Whole Number Operations** (long division, multi-digit multiplication). No calculators allowed on the CAAT, so we need to dust off those mental gears!
- **Day 4: Reading — Finding the Anchor**
  - Practice identifying the **Main Idea**. Read a short news article and summarize it in exactly one sentence. If you can't summarize it, you didn't catch the anchor.
- **Day 5: Vocabulary — Word Surgery**
  - Study **Prefixes and Suffixes** (e.g., *un-*, *re-*, *-ology*). If you know the parts, you can "perform surgery" on a word you've never seen before to find its meaning.
- **Day 6: Math — The "Parts of a Whole"**
  - Fractions and Decimals. Practice converting $1/4$ to 0.25. This is where "Big Prep" usually loses people, so keep it simple.
- **Day 7: Rest & Reflect**
  - Review your Pocket Glossary. No new learning today.

Week 2: Building Stamina & Strategy
Focus: Tackling the tougher stuff like word problems and longer passages.
- **Day 8: Math — The Dreaded Word Problems**
  o We call this "Math in English." Practice translating words into equations. Keywords: "Of" means multiply, "Sum" means add.
- **Day 9: Reading — Reading Between the Lines**
  o **Inference questions.** These ask what the author *implies*. Practice asking, "What is the author trying to tell me without actually saying it?"
- **Day 10: Vocabulary — Context Clues**
  o Practice sentences where a word is missing. Don't look at the choices yet—guess what fits, then find the match.
- **Day 11: Math — Percentages and Ratios**
  o Think of these as "Retail Math." How much is a 15% tip? How do you split a 2:1 ratio?
- **Day 12: Reading — Purpose and Tone**
  o Is the author angry? Persuasive? Just giving facts? Identifying the "vibe" helps you eliminate wrong answers fast.
- **Day 13: Math — The "X" Factor**
  o Basic Algebra. Solving for x in simple equations (e.g., $2x + 5 = 11$). Keep it grounded—algebra is just a puzzle with a missing piece.
- **Day 14: Mid-Point Check**
  o Take a timed 20-minute mini-quiz on each section. See if the "clock pressure" changes your performance.

Week 3: The Finish Line
Focus: Speed, accuracy, and confidence.
- **Day 15: Math — Geometry and Measurement**
    - Area, perimeter, and basic shapes. Remember: Perimeter is the fence; Area is the grass.
- **Day 16: Reading — Technical Passages**
    - Practice reading instructions or "drier" non-fiction. CAAT loves to throw a manual or a report at you.
- **Day 17: Vocabulary — Final Polish**
    - Review your full Pocket Glossary. Focus on "Commonly Confused Words" (their/there/they're).
- **Day 18: Math — Data and Graphs**
    - Reading pie charts and bar graphs. Don't let the colors distract you—look at the legend first.
- **Day 19: The Full Dress Rehearsal**
    - Take a full-length, timed practice test. Sit at a desk, no phone, just you and the paper.
- **Day 20: The "Clean Up"**
    - Review only the questions you got wrong on Day 19. Don't start new topics now.
- **Day 21: Mental Prep**
    - Pack your bag (ID, pencils, water). Do a quick visualization of walking into the room and feeling calm. You've done the work.

Tips for making a schedule

Once you make a schedule, stick with it! Make your study sessions reasonable. If you make a study schedule and don't stick with it, you set yourself up for failure. Instead, schedule study sessions that are a bit shorter and set yourself up for success! Make sure your study sessions are do-able. Studying is hard work, but after you pass, you can party and take a break!

Schedule breaks. Breaks are just as important as study time. Work out a rotation of studying and breaks that works for you.

Build up study time. If you find it hard to sit still and study for 1 hour straight through, build up to it. Start with 20 minutes, and then take a break. Once you get used to 20-minute study sessions, increase the time to 30 minutes. Gradually work you way up to 1 hour.

How to Make a Study Plan and Schedule
https://www.test-preparation.ca/make-study-plan/

40 minutes to 1 hour is optimal. Studying for longer than this is tiring and not productive. Studying for shorter isn't long enough to be productive.

Studying Math. Studying Math is different from studying other subjects because you use a different part of your brain. The best way to study math is to practice everyday. This will train your mind to think in a mathematical way. If you miss a day or days, the mathematical mind-set is gone, and you have to start all over again to build it up.

More Info on Making a Study Plan

How to study math

https://www.test-preparation.ca/study-math/

How to Study
For more information, see our How to Study Guide at
https://www.test-preparation.ca/learning-study/

Flash Cards - The Complete Guide

https://www.test-preparation.ca/flash-cards/

Getting the Most from Practice Questions

Taking a practice test is probably the best way to prepare for a test.

Quick tips to get the most from practice questions:

Simulate Test Conditions

- Choose a quiet, distraction-free environment.

- Use a timer and allow just under 1 minute per question.

- Avoid using notes or online texts

Take it seriously -

- Treat the practice test as if it's the real exam -

- Familiarize yourself with the format and topics - this will reduce anxiety.

-

-

After Completing a Practice Test

Reviewing your work after you take a practice test is critical.

Immediate Review

- Make a note of any questions you found challenging or topics that felt unfamiliar or difficult.

- How was your time management?

- Overall comfort during the test?

Do a Thorough Review

- Go over your answers focusing on correct and incorrect answers.

- For incorrect answers, identify misunderstandings knowledge gaps or problem subject areas - here is where you need to spend your study time.

Look for Patterns

- Look for recurring themes in your errors to pinpoint specific areas needing improvement.

- Assess whether mistakes were due to content gaps, misinterpretation of questions, or time constraints.

Reading Between the Lines: Mastering the Message

Welcome to the Reading Comprehension Section
Before we dive into the deep end, let's take a second to talk about what's ahead. This chapter is divided into two parts: a Self-Assessment (to see where you stand) and Tutorials (to help you get where you need to be).

Think of the tutorials as a "refresher course." We've designed them to cover the big ideas you'll see on the CAAT, but they aren't meant to be a full college semester. Most of you already have the skills—we're just here to help you dust them off. If something feels a bit tricky, don't sweat it! That just means it's a good time to slow down or look for a little extra help.

Why start with a Self-Assessment?
We aren't just giving you more "homework." This quiz is a tool to help you:

Spot your strengths: See what you already know so you don't waste time on it.

Find the "potholes": Identify exactly which areas need a bit more grease.

Get used to the rhythm: The CAAT has its own way of asking things; this helps you get comfortable with that style.

Extra practice: This assessment is basically a third practice test—the more "reps" you get, the better you'll be on game day.

The Clock and the Questions
On the real CAAT, you'll have 50 questions and only 40 minutes. That's a brisk pace!

For this self-assessment, we've picked 15 questions. If you want to simulate the real test, try to finish them in about 12 minutes. But listen—if you're just starting out and want to focus on accuracy first, feel free to ignore the timer. We're building confidence here, not just speed.

A quick heads-up: Nobody (including us!) knows exactly which stories or questions will be on the test this year. They change them all the time. But we've spent years "triple-checking" the CAAT requirements to make sure these questions cover the same ground. If you can handle these, you can handle the real thing.

Checking Your Score
Once you've finished the 15 questions, see how you stack up. Here's my honest take on what your score means:

Score	What it means...
75% – 100%	**Excellent.** You've got this down pat! You're ready to move forward.
50% – 75%	**Good.** You've got the basics, but there's room to sharpen the saw. I'd suggest a quick skim of the tutorials to pick up a few extra points.
25% – 50%	**Below Average.** You might be struggling with how the questions are framed. Take a beat, go through the tutorials carefully, and try the quiz again in a few days.
Under 25%	**Needs Work.** Don't get discouraged! It just means we need to build a stronger foundation. Spend some quality time with the tutorials before moving on to the full practice tests.

After taking the Self-Assessment, use the table above to assess your understanding. If you scored low, read through the Tutorial, Help with Reading Comprehension, and if you need more practice, see Multiple Choice Secrets at

www.multiple-choice.ca

Reading Between the Lines

Self-Assessment Answer Sheet

	A	B	C	D
1	○	○	○	○
2	○	○	○	○
3	○	○	○	○
4	○	○	○	○
5	○	○	○	○
6	○	○	○	○
7	○	○	○	○
8	○	○	○	○
9	○	○	○	○
10	○	○	○	○
11	○	○	○	○
12	○	○	○	○
13	○	○	○	○
14	○	○	○	○
15	○	○	○	○

Directions: The following questions are based on several reading passages. Each passage is followed by a series of questions. Read each passage carefully, and then answer the questions based on it. You may reread the passage as often as you wish. When you have finished answering the questions based on one passage, go right onto the next passage. Choose the best answer based on the information given and implied.

Questions 1 – 4 refer to the following passage.

Passage 1 - Who Was Anne Frank?

You may have heard mention of the word Holocaust in your History or English classes. The Holocaust took place from 1939-1945. It was an attempt by the Nazi party to purify the human race, by eliminating Jews, Gypsies, Catholics, homosexuals and others they deemed inferior to their "perfect" Aryan race. The Nazis used Concentration Camps, which were sometimes used as Death Camps, to exterminate the people they held in the camps. The saddest fact about the Holocaust was the over one million children under the age of sixteen died in a Nazi concentration camp. Just a few weeks before World War II was over, Anne Frank was one of those children to die.

Before the Nazi party began its persecution of the Jews, Anne Frank had a happy life. She was born in June of 1929. In June of 1942, for her 13th birthday, she was given a simple present which would go onto impact the lives of millions of people around the world. That gift was a small red diary that she called Kitty. This diary was to become Anne's most treasured possession when she and her family hid from the Nazis in a secret annex above her father's office building in Amsterdam.

For 25 months, Anne, her sister Margot, her parents, another family, and an elderly Jewish dentist hid from the Nazis in this tiny annex. They were never permitted to go outside, and their food and supplies were brought to them by Miep Gies and her husband, who did not believe in the Nazi persecution of the Jews. It was a very difficult life for young Anne and she used Kitty as an outlet to describe her life in hiding. After 2 years, Anne and her family were betrayed and arrested by the Nazis. To this day, nobody is exactly sure who betrayed the Frank family and the other annex residents. Anne, her mother, and her sister were separated from Otto Frank, Anne's father. Then, Anne and Margot were separated from their mother. In March of 1945, Margot Frank died of starvation in a Concentration Camp. A few days later, at the age of 15, Anne Frank died of typhus. Of all the people who hid in the Annex, only Otto Frank survived the Holocaust.

Otto Frank returned to the Annex after World War II. It was there that he found Kitty, filled with Anne's thoughts and feelings about being a persecuted Jewish girl. Otto Frank had Anne's diary published in 1947 and it has remained continuously in print ever since. Today, the diary has been published in over 55 languages and more than 24 million copies have been sold around the world. The Diary of Anne Frank tells the story of a brave young woman who tried to see the good in all people.

1. From the context clues in the passage, what does the word Annex mean?

    a. Attic

    b. Bedroom

    c. Basement

    d. Kitchen

2. Why do you think Anne's diary has been published in 55 languages?

    a. So everyone could understand it.

    b. So people around the world could learn more about the horrors of the Holocaust.

    c. Because Anne was Jewish but hid in Amsterdam and died in Germany.

    d. Because Otto Frank spoke many languages.

3. From the description of Anne and Margot's deaths in the passage, what can we assume typhus is?

    a. The same as starving to death.

    b. An infection the Germans gave to Anne.

    c. A disease Anne caught in the concentration camp.

    d. Poison gas used by the Germans to kill Anne.

4. In the third paragraph, what does the word outlet mean?

    a. A place to plug things into the wall

    b. A store where Miep bought cheap supplies for the Frank family

    c. A hiding space similar to an Annex

    d. A place where Anne could express her private thoughts.

Questions 5 – 8 refer to the following passage.

Passage 2 - Was Dr. Seuss A Real Doctor?

A favorite author for over 100 years, Theodor Seuss Geisel was born on March 2, 1902. Today, we celebrate the birthday of the famous "Dr. Seuss" by hosting Read Across America events throughout the March. School children around the country celebrate the "Doctor's" birthday by making hats, giving presentations and holding read aloud circles featuring some of Dr. Seuss' most famous books.

But who was Dr. Seuss? Did he go to medical school? Where was his office? You may be surprised to know that Theodor Seuss Geisel was not a medical doctor at all. He took on the nickname Dr. Seuss when he became a noted children's book author. He earned the nickname because people said his books were "as good as medicine." All these years later, his nickname has lasted and he is known as Dr. Seuss all across the world.

Reading Between the Lines

Think back to when you were a young child. Did you ever want to try "green eggs and ham?" Did you try to "Hop on Pop?" Do you remember learning about the environment from a creature called The Lorax? Of course, you must recall one of Seuss' most famous characters; that green Grinch who stole Christmas. These stories were all written by Dr. Seuss and featured his signature rhyming words and letters. They also featured made up words to enhance his rhyme scheme and even though many of his characters were made up, they sure seem real to us today.

And what of his "signature" book, The Cat in the Hat? You must remember that cat and Thing One and Thing Two from your childhood. Did you know that in the early 1950's there was a growing concern in America that children were not becoming avid readers? This was, book publishers thought, because children found books dull and uninteresting. An intelligent publisher sent Dr. Seuss a book of words that he thought all children should learn as young readers. Dr. Seuss wrote his famous story The Cat in the Hat, using those words. We can see, over the decades, just how much influence his writing has had on very young children. That is why we celebrate this doctor's birthday each March.

5. What does the word "avid" mean in the last paragraph?

   a. Good

   b. Interested

   c. Slow

   d. Fast

6. What can we infer from the statement " His books were like medicine?"

   a. His books made people feel better

   b. His books were in doctor's office waiting rooms

   c. His books took away fevers

   d. His books left a funny taste in readers' mouths.

7. Why is the publisher in the last paragraph called "intelligent?"

   a. The publisher knew how to read.

   b. The publisher knew kids did not like to read.

   c. The publisher knew Dr. Seuss would be able to create a book that sold well.

   d. The publisher knew that Dr. Seuss would be able to write a book that would get young children interested in reading.

8. The theme of this passage is

   a. Dr. Seuss was not a doctor.

   b. Dr. Seuss influenced the lives of generations of young children.

   c. Dr. Seuss wrote rhyming books.

   d. Dr. Suess' birthday is a good day to read a book.

Questions 9 - 12 refer to the following passage.

Keeping Tropical Fish

Keeping tropical fish at home or in your office used to be very popular. Today, interest has declined, but it remains as rewarding and relaxing a hobby as ever. Ask any tropical fish hobbyist, and you will hear how soothing and relaxing watching colorful fish live their lives in the aquarium. If you are considering keeping tropical fish as pets, here is a list of basic equipment you will need.

A filter is essential for keeping your aquarium clean and your fish alive and healthy. There are different types and sizes of filters and the right size for you depends on the size of the aquarium and the level of stocking. Generally, you need a filter with a 3 to 5 times turn over rate per hour. This means that the water in the tank should go through the filter about 3 to 5 times per hour.

Most tropical fish do well in water temperatures ranging between 24° C and 26° C, though each has its own ideal water temperature. A heater with a thermostat is necessary to regulate the water temperature. Some heaters are submersible and others are not, so check carefully before you buy.

Lights are also necessary, and come in a large variety of types, strengths and sizes. A light source is necessary for plants in the tank to photo-synthesize and give the tank a more attractive appearance. Even if you plan to use plastic plants, the fish still require light, although here you can use a lower strength light source.

A hood is necessary to keep dust, dirt and unwanted materials out of the tank. Sometimes the hood can also help prevent evaporation. Another requirement is aquarium gravel. This will improve the aesthetics of the aquarium and is necessary if you plan to have real plants.

9. What is the general tone of this article?

   a. Formal

   b. Informal

   c. Technical

   d. Opinion

10. Which of the following cannot be inferred?

   a. Gravel is good for aquarium plants.

   b. Fewer people have aquariums in their office than at home.

   c. The larger the tank, the larger the filter required.

   d. None of the above.

11. What evidence does the author provide to support their claim that aquarium lights are necessary?

    a. Plants require light.

    b. Fish and plants require light.

    c. The author does not provide evidence for this statement.

    d. Aquarium lights make the aquarium more attractive.

12. Which of the following is an opinion?

    a. Filter with a 3 to 5 times turn over rate per hour are required.

    b. Aquarium gravel improves the aesthetics of the aquarium.

    c. An aquarium hood keeps dust, dirt and unwanted materials out of the tank.

    d. Each type of tropical fish has its own ideal water temperature.

Questions 13 - 15 refer to the following passage.

The Civil War

The Civil War began on April 12, 1861. The first shots of the Civil War were fired in Fort Sumter, South Carolina. Even though more American lives were lost in the Civil War than in any other war, not one person died on that first day. The war began because eleven Southern states seceded from the Union and tried to start their own government, The Confederate States of America.

Why did the states secede? The issue of slavery was a primary cause of the Civil War. The eleven southern states relied heavily on their slaves to foster their farming and plantation lifestyles. The northern states, many of whom had already abolished slavery, did not feel that the southern states should have slaves. The north wanted to free all the slaves and President Lincoln's goal was to both end slavery and preserve the Union. He had Congress declare war on the Confederacy on April 14, 1862. For four long, blood soaked years, the North and South fought.

From 1861 to mid 1863, it seemed as if the South would win this war. However, on July 1, 1863, an epic three day battle was waged on a field in Gettysburg, Pennsylvania. Gettysburg is remembered for being the bloodiest battle in American history. At the end of the three days, the North turned the tide of the war in their favor. The North then went on to dominate the South for the remainder of the war. Another famous event is General Sherman's "March to The Sea," where he famously led the Union Army through Georgia and the Carolinas, burning and destroying everything in their path.

In 1865, the Union army invaded and captured the Confederate capital of Richmond Virginia. Robert E. Lee, leader of the Confederacy surrendered to General Ulysses S. Grant, leader of the Union forces, on April 9, 1865. The Civil War was over and the Union was preserved.

13. What does secede mean?

    a. To break away from

    b. To accomplish

    c. To join

    d. To lose

14. Which of the following statements summarizes a FACT from the passage?

    a. Congress declared war and then the Battle of Fort Sumter began.

    b. Congress declared war after shots were fired at Fort Sumter.

    c. President Lincoln was pro slavery

    d. President Lincoln was at Fort Sumter with Congress

15. Which event finally led the Confederacy to surrender?

    a. The battle of Gettysburg
    b. The battle of Bull Run
    c. The invasion of the confederate capital of Richmond
    d. Sherman's March to the Sea

Reading Between the Lines

Answer Key

1. A
We know that an annex is like an attic because the text states the annex was above Otto Frank's building.

Choice B is incorrect because an office building doesn't have bedrooms. Choice C is incorrect because a basement would be below the office building. Choice D is incorrect because there would not be a kitchen in an office building.

2. B
The diary has been published in 55 languages so people all over the world can learn about Anne. That is why the passage says it has been continuously in print.

Choice A is incorrect because it is too vague. Choice C is incorrect because it was published after Anne died and she did not write in all three languages. Choice D is incorrect because the passage does not give us any information about what languages Otto Frank spoke.

3. C
Use the process of elimination to figure this out.

Choice A cannot be the correct answer because, otherwise the passage would have simply said that Anne and Margot both died of starvation. Choices B and D cannot be correct because, if the Germans had done something specifically to murder Anne, the passage would have stated that directly. By the process of elimination, choice C has to be the correct answer.

4. D
We can figure this out using context clues. The paragraph is talking about Anne's diary and so, outlet in this instance is a place where Anne can pour her feelings.

Choice A is incorrect answer. That is the literal meaning of the word outlet and the passage is using the figurative meaning. Choice B is incorrect because that is the secondary literal meaning of the word outlet, as in an outlet mall. Again, we are looking for figurative meaning. Choice C is incorrect because there are no clues in the text to support that answer.

5. B
When someone is avid about something that means they are highly interested in the subject. The context clues are dull and boring, because they define the opposite of avid.

6. A
The author is using a simile to compare the books to medicine. Medicine is what you take when you want to feel better. They are suggesting that if you want to feel good, they should read Dr. Seuss' books.

Choice B is incorrect because there is no mention of a doctor's office. Choice C is incorrect because it is using the literal meaning of medicine and the author is using medicine in a figurative way. Choice D is incorrect because it makes no sense. We know not to eat books.

7. D
The publisher is described as intelligent because he knew to get in touch with a famous author to develop a book that children would be interested in reading.

Choice A is incorrect because we can assume that all book publishers must know how to read. Choice B is incorrect because it says in the article that more than one publisher was concerned whether children liked to read. Choice D is incorrect because there is no mention in the article about how well The Cat in the Hat sold when it was first published.

8. B
The passage describes in detail how Dr. Seuss had a great effect on the lives of children through his writing. It names several of his books, tells how he helped children become avid readers and explains his style of writing.

Choice A is incorrect because that is just one single fact about the passage. Choice C is incorrect because that is just one single fact about the passage. Choice D is incorrect because that is just one single fact about the passage. Again, choice B is correct because it encompasses ALL the facts in the passage, not just one single fact.

9. B
The general tone is informal.

10. B
The statement, "Fewer people have aquariums in their office than at home," cannot be inferred from this article.

11. C
The author does not provide evidence for this statement.

12. B
The following statement is an opinion, " Aquarium gravel improves the aesthetics of the aquarium."

13. A
Secede means to break away from because the 11 states wanted to leave the United States and form their own country.

Choice B is incorrect because the states were not accomplishing anything. Choice C is incorrect because the states were trying to leave the USA not join it. Choice D is incorrect because the states seceded before they lost the war.

14. B
Look at the dates in the passage. The shots were fired on April 12 and Congress declared war on April 14.

Choice C is incorrect because the passage states that Lincoln was against slavery. Choice D is incorrect because it never mentions who was or was not at Fort Sumter.

15. C
The passage states that Lee surrendered to Grant after the capture of the capital of the Confederacy, which is Richmond.

Choice A is incorrect because the war continued for 2 years after Gettysburg. Choice B is incorrect because that battle is not mentioned in the passage. Choice D is incorrect because the capture of the capital occurred after the march to the sea.

Help with Reading Comprehension

At first sight, reading comprehension tests look challenging especially if you are given long essays to answer only two to three questions. While reading, you might notice your attention waning, or feeling sleepy. Do not be discouraged because there are various tactics and long range strategies that make comprehending even long, boring essays easier.

Your friends before your foes. It is always best to start with essays or passages with familiar subjects rather than those with unfamiliar ones. This approach applies the same logic as tackling easy questions before hard ones. Skip passages that do not interest you and leave them for later.

Don't use 'special' reading techniques. This is not the time for speed-reading or anything like that – just plain ordinary reading – not too slow and not too fast.

Read through the entire passage and the questions before you do anything. Many students try reading the questions first and then looking for answers in the passage thinking this approach is more efficient. What these students do not realize is that it is often hard to navigate in unfamiliar roads. If you do not familiarize yourself with the passage first, looking for answers become not only time-consuming but also dangerous because you might miss the context of the answer you are looking for. If you read the questions first you will only confuse yourself and lose valuable time.

Familiarize yourself with reading comprehension questions. If you are familiar with the common types of reading comprehension questions, you are able to take note of important parts of the passage, saving time. There are six major kinds of reading comprehension questions.

- **Main Idea** - Questions that ask for the central thought or significance of the passage.

- **Specific Details** - Questions that asks for explicitly stated ideas.

- **Drawing Inferences** - Questions that ask for a statement's intended meaning.

- **Tone or Attitude** - Questions that test your ability to sense the emotional state of the author.

- **Context Meaning** – Questions that ask for the meaning of a word depending on the context.

- **Technique** – Questions that ask for the method of organization or the writing style of the author.

Read. Read. Read. The best preparation for reading comprehension tests is always to read, read and read. If you are not used to reading lengthy passages, you will probably lose concentration. Increase your attention span by making a habit out of reading.

Reading Comprehension tests become less daunting when you have trained yourself to read and understand fast. Always remember that it is easier to understand passages you are interested in. Do not read through passages hastily. Make mental notes of ideas you may be asked.

Reading Comprehension Strategy

When facing the reading comprehension section of a standardized test, you need a strategy to be successful. You want to keep several steps in mind:

- First, make a note of the time and the number of sections. Time your work accordingly. Typically, four to five minutes per section is sufficient. Second, read the directions for each selection thoroughly before beginning (and listen well to any additional verbal instructions, as they will often clarify obscure or confusing written guidelines). You must know exactly how to do what you're about to do!

- Now you're ready to begin reading the selection. Read the passage carefully, noting significant characters or events on a scratch sheet of paper or underlining on the test sheet. Many students find making a basic list in the margins helpful. Quickly jot down or underline one-word summaries of characters, notable happenings, numbers, or key ideas. This will help you better retain information and focus wandering thoughts. Remember, however, that your main goal in doing this is to find the information that answers the questions. Even if you find the passage interesting, remember your goal and work fast but stay on track.

- Now read the question and all the choices. Now you have read the passage, have a general idea of the main ideas, and have marked the important points. Read the question and all the choices. Never choose an answer without reading them all! Questions are often designed to confuse – stay focussed and clear. Usually the answer choices will focus on one or two facts or inferences from the passage. Keep these clear in your mind.

- Search for the answer. With a very general idea of what the different choices are, go back to the passage and scan for the relevant information. Watch for big words, unusual or unique words. These make your job easier as you can scan the text for the particular word.

- Mark the Answer. Now you have the key information that the question is looking for. Go back to the question, quickly scan the choices and mark the correct one.

Understand and practice the different types of standardized reading comprehension tests. See the list above for the different types. Typically, there will be several questions dealing with facts from the selection, a couple more inference questions dealing with logical consequences of those facts, and periodically an application-oriented question surfaces to force you to make connections with what you already know. Some students prefer to answer the questions as listed, and feel classifying the question and then ordering is wasting precious time. Other students prefer to answer the different types of questions in order of how easy or difficult they are. The choice is yours and do whatever works for you. If you want to try answering in order of difficulty, here is a recommended order, answer fact questions first; they're easily found within the passage. Tackle inference problems next, after re-reading the question(s) as many times as you need to. Application or 'best guess' questions usually take the longest, so, save them for last.

Use the practice tests to try out both ways of answering and see what works for you.

For more help with reading comprehension, see Multiple Choice Secrets at www.multiple-choice.ca.

Main Idea and Supporting Details

Identifying the main idea, topic and supporting details in a passage can feel like an overwhelming task. The passages used for standardized tests can be boring and seem difficult - Test writers don't use interesting passages or ones that talk about things most people are familiar with. Despite these obstacles, all passages and paragraphs will have the information you need to answer the questions.

The topic of a passage or paragraph is its subject. It's the general idea and can be summed up in a word or short phrase. On some standardized tests, there is a short description of the passage if it's taken from a longer work. Make sure you read the description as it might state the topic of the passage. If not, read the passage and ask yourself, "Who or what is this about?" For example:

> Over the years, school uniforms have been hotly debated. Arguments are made that students have the right to show individuality and express themselves by choosing their own clothes. However, this brings up social and academic issues. Some kids cannot afford to wear the clothes they like and might be bullied by the "better dressed" students. With attention drawn to clothes and the individual,

students will lose focus on class work and the reason they are in school. School uniforms should be mandatory.

Ask: What is this paragraph about?

Topic: school uniforms

Once you have the topic, it's easier to find the main idea. The main idea is a specific statement telling what the writer wants you to understand about the topic. Writers usually state the main idea as a thesis statement. If you're looking for the main idea of a single paragraph, the main idea is called the topic sentence and will probably be the first or last sentence. If you're looking for the main idea of an entire passage, look for the thesis statement in either the first or last paragraph. The main idea is usually restated in the conclusion. To find the main idea of a passage or paragraph, follow these steps:

1. Find the topic.

2. Ask yourself, "What point is the author trying to make about the topic?"

3. Create your own sentence summarizing the author's point.

4. Look in the text for the sentence closest in meaning to yours.

Look at the example paragraph again. It's already established that the topic of the paragraph is school uniforms. What is the main idea/topic sentence?

Ask: "What point is the author trying to make about school uniforms?"

Summary: Students should wear school uniforms.

Topic sentence: School uniforms should be mandatory.

Main Idea: School uniforms should be mandatory.

Each paragraph offers supporting details to explain the main idea. The details could be facts or reasons, but they will always answer a question about the main idea. What? Where? Why? When? How? How much/many? Look at the example paragraph again. You'll notice that more than one sentence answers a question about the main idea. These are the supporting details.

Main Idea: School uniforms should be mandatory.

Ask: Why? Some kids cannot afford to wear clothes they like and could be bullied by the "better dressed" kids. Supporting Detail

With attention drawn to clothes and the individual, Students will lose focus on class work and the reason they are in school. Supporting Detail

What if the author doesn't state the main idea in a topic sentence? The passage will have an implied main idea. It's not as difficult to find as it might seem. Paragraphs are always organized around ideas. To find an implied main idea, you need to know the topic and then find the relationship between the supporting details. Ask yourself, "What is the point the author is making about the relationship between the details?."

> Cocoa is what makes chocolate good for you. Chocolate comes in many varieties. These delectable flavors include milk chocolate, dark chocolate, semi-sweet, and white chocolate.

Ask: What is this paragraph about?

Topic: Chocolate

Ask: What? Where? Why? When? How? How much/many?

Supporting details: Chocolate is good for you because it is made of cocoa, Chocolate is delicious, Chocolate comes in different delicious flavors

Ask: What is the relationship between the details and what is the author's point?

Main Idea: Chocolate is good because it is healthy and it tastes good.

Testing Tips for Main Idea Questions

1. Skim the questions – not the answer choices - before reading the passage.

2. Questions about main idea might use the words "theme," "generalization," or "purpose."

3. Save questions about the main idea for last. Questions can often be found in order in the passage.

3. Underline topic sentences in the passage. Most tests allow you to write in your test booklet.

4. Answer the question in your own words before looking at the answer choices. Then match your answer with an answer choice.

5. Cross out incorrect answer choices immediately to prevent confusion.

6. If two of the answer choices mean the same thing but use different words, they are BOTH incorrect.

7. If a question asks about the whole passage, cross out the answer choices that apply only to part of it.

8. If only part of the information is correct, that answer choice is incorrect.

9. An answer choice that is too broad is incorrect. All information needs to be backed up by the passage.

10. Answer choices with extreme wording are usually incorrect.

Reading Quick Tips

QUICK TIPS

Active Reading: highlight key points, underlining or marking key information, and making marginal notes.

Preview the Questions: Before reading the passage, quickly look skim the questions to identify the information you need to focus on. This technique helps in pinpointing relevant details during your reading.

Summarize: After reading each paragraph, briefly summarize its main idea in your own words.

Watch Text Structure: Look at how the passage is organized — cause-effect, compare-contrast, or problem-solution.

Meaning in Context: If you don't recognize a word, Look for clues in the surrounding sentences to infer the meaning. Generally, you don't have to know the exact meaning.

Eliminate Wrong Answers: Elimination is the most powerful strategy for multiple-choice. Eliminating clearly wrong options improves the odds of selecting the correct answer. More on Multiple Choice Strategy here www.multiple-choice.ca

Refer Back to the Passage: Always base your answers on information directly in the text. Don't rely on prior knowledge or make assumptions

Drawing Inferences And Conclusions

Video Version of this Tutorial
https://www.test-preparation.ca/making-inferences/

Drawing inferences and making conclusions happens all the time. In fact, you probably do it every time you read—sometimes without even realizing it! For example, remember the first time you saw the movie "The Lion King." When you meet Scar for the first time, he is trapping a helpless mouse with his sharp claws preparing to eat it. When you see this action you guess that Scar is going to be a bad character in the movie. Nothing appeared to tell you this. No caption came across the bottom of the screen that said "Bad Guy." No red arrow pointed to Scar and said "Evil Lion." No, you made an inference about his character based on the context clue you were given. You do the same thing when you read!

When you draw an inference or make a conclusion you are doing the same thing, you are making an educated guess based on the hints the author gives you. We call these hints "context clues." Scar trapping the innocent mouse is the context clue about Scar's character.

Usually you are making inferences and drawing conclusions the entire time that you are reading. Whether you realize it or not, you are constantly making educated guesses based on context clues. Think about a time you were reading a book and something happened that you were expecting to happen. You're not psychic! Actually, you were picking up on the context clues and making inferences about what was going to happen next!

Let's try an easy example. Read the following sentences and answer the questions at the end of the passage.

Shelly really likes to help people. She loves her job because she gets to help people every single day. However, Shelly has to work long hours and she can get called in the middle of the night for emergencies. She wears a white lab coat at work and usually she carries a stethoscope.

What is most likely Shelly's job?

    a. Musician

    b. Lawyer

    c. Doctor

    d. Teacher

This probably seemed easy. Drawing inferences isn't always this simple, but it is the same basic principle. How did you know Shelly was a doctor? She helps people, she works long hours, she wears a white lab coat, and she gets called in for emergencies at night. Context Clues! Nowhere in the paragraph did it say Shelly was a doctor, but you were able to draw that conclusion based on the information provided in the paragraph. This is how it's done!

There is a catch, though. Remember that when you draw inferences based on reading, you should only use the information given to you by the author. Sometimes it is easy for us to make conclusions based on knowledge that is already in our mind—but that can lead you to drawing an incorrect inference. For example, let's pretend there is a bully at your school named Brent. Now let's say you read a story and the main character's name is Brent. You could NOT infer that the character in the story is a bully just because his name is Brent. You should only use the information given to you by the author to avoid drawing the wrong conclusion.

Let's try another example. Read the passage below and answer the question.

Social media is an extremely popular new form of connecting and communicating over the internet. Since Facebook's original launch in 2004, millions of people have joined in the social media craze. In fact, it is estimated that almost 75% of all internet users aged 18 and older use some form of social media. Facebook started at Harvard University as a way to get students connected. However, it quickly grew into a worldwide phenomenon and today, the founder of Facebook, Mark Zuckerberg has an estimated net worth of 28.5 billion dollars.

Facebook is not the only social media platform, though. Other sites such as Twitter, Instagram, and Snapchat have since been invented and are quickly becoming just as popular! Many social media users actually use more than one type of social media. Furthermore, most social media sites have created mobile apps that allow people to connect via social media virtually anywhere in the world!

What is the most likely reason that other social media sites like Twitter and Instagram were created?

    a. Professors at Harvard University made it a class project.

    b. Facebook was extremely popular and other people thought they could also be successful by designing social media sites.

    c. Facebook was not connecting enough people.

    d. Mark Zuckerberg paid people to invent new social media sites because he wanted lots of competition.

Here, the correct answer is B. Facebook was extremely popular and other people thought they could also be successful by designing social media sites. How do we know this? What are the context clues? Take a look at the first paragraph. What do we know based on this paragraph? Well, one sentence refers to Facebook's original launch. This suggests that Facebook was one of the first social media sites. In addition, we know that the founder of Facebook has been extremely successful and is worth billions of dollars. From this we can infer that other people wanted to imitate Facebook's idea and become just as successful as Mark Zuckerberg.

Let's go through the other answers. If you chose A, it might be because Facebook started at Harvard University, so you drew the conclusion that all other social media sites were also started at Harvard University. However, there is no mention of class projects, professors, or students designing social media. So there doesn't seem to be enough support for choice A.

If you chose C, you might have been drawing your own conclusions based on outside information. Maybe none of your friends are on Facebook, so you made an inference that Facebook didn't connect enough people, so more sites were invented. Or maybe you think the people who connect on Facebook are too old, so you don't think Facebook connects enough people your age. This might be true, but remember inferences should be drawn from the information the author gives you!

If you chose D, you might be using the information that Mark Zuckerberg is worth over 28 billion dollars. It would be easy for him to pay others to design new sites, but remember, you need to use context clues! He is very wealthy, but that statement was giving you information about how successful Facebook was—not suggesting that he paid others to design more sites!

So remember, drawing inferences and conclusions is simply about using the information you are given to make an educated guess. You do this every single day so don't let this concept scare you. Look for the context clues, make sure they support your claim, and you'll be able to make accurate inferences and conclusions!

The Toolbox: Everyday Math for the Exam

Number Operations: Getting Back to the Basics
Welcome to the Number Operations section. If it's been a few years (or a few decades) since you last did long division or wrestled with a fraction, don't worry—you're in good company.

This chapter includes a Self-Assessment to help you find your footing and Tutorials to polish up your skills. We aren't trying to teach a four-year high school math curriculum here; we're focusing on the specific "gears" you need to get moving for the CAAT. If you hit a wall in the tutorials, don't beat yourself up. It just means it might be time to reach out for a little extra coaching or find a supplemental workbook.

The Math Self-Assessment
Think of this as a "check-up" for your math skills. Use it to:

- **Spot the "Rust":** Figure out if you're great at decimals but a bit shaky on ratios.
- **Build Your Plan:** Focus your study time where it actually matters.
- **Get Used to the CAAT Style:** The exam covers decimals, whole numbers, fractions, metric conversions, percentages, and basic algebra. This assessment gives you a taste of all of them.

- **Bonus Practice:** Between this and the main practice tests, you're getting a lot of "miles" under your belt before the real thing.
-

Timing and Strategy

On the real CAAT, you'll face **40 questions in 40 minutes**. That's "a minute a mile," so to speak.

Our self-assessment also has **40 questions**. If you're feeling brave, set a timer for 40 minutes to see how you handle the pace. If you're just getting back into the swing of things, feel free to ignore the clock for now. Accuracy is more important than speed when you're first starting out at the kitchen table. Note: Just like the reading section, these aren't the exact questions from the official exam—nobody has those! But we've spent years in the classroom and at the publisher's desk making sure these problems mirror the difficulty and "flavor" of the real CAAT.

Checking Your Score

Once you've finished the 15 questions, see how you stack up. Here's my honest take on what your score means:

Score	What it means...
75% – 100%	**Excellent.** You've got this down pat! You're ready to move forward.
50% – 75%	**Good.** You've got the basics, but there's room to sharpen the saw. I'd suggest a quick skim of the tutorials to pick up a few extra points.
25% – 50%	**Below Average.** You might be struggling with how the questions are framed. Take a beat, go through the tutorials carefully, and try the quiz again in a few days.
Under 25%	**Needs Work.** Don't get discouraged! It just means we need to build a stronger foundation. Spend some quality time with the tutorials before moving on to the full practice tests.

PASS THE CAAT!

Answer Sheet

	A	B	C	D	E		A	B	C	D	E
1	○	○	○	○	○	21	○	○	○	○	○
2	○	○	○	○	○	22	○	○	○	○	○
3	○	○	○	○	○	23	○	○	○	○	○
4	○	○	○	○	○	24	○	○	○	○	○
5	○	○	○	○	○	25	○	○	○	○	○
6	○	○	○	○	○	26	○	○	○	○	○
7	○	○	○	○	○	27	○	○	○	○	○
8	○	○	○	○	○	28	○	○	○	○	○
9	○	○	○	○	○	29	○	○	○	○	○
10	○	○	○	○	○	30	○	○	○	○	○
11	○	○	○	○	○	31	○	○	○	○	○
12	○	○	○	○	○	32	○	○	○	○	○
13	○	○	○	○	○	33	○	○	○	○	○
14	○	○	○	○	○	34	○	○	○	○	○
15	○	○	○	○	○	35	○	○	○	○	○
16	○	○	○	○	○	36	○	○	○	○	○
17	○	○	○	○	○	37	○	○	○	○	○
18	○	○	○	○	○	38	○	○	○	○	○
19	○	○	○	○	○	39	○	○	○	○	○
20	○	○	○	○	○	40	○	○	○	○	○

Number Operations

1. 389 + 454 =

    a. 853
    b. 833
    c. 843
    d. 863

2. 9,177 + 7,204 =

    a. 16,4712
    b. 16,371
    c. 16,381
    d. 15,412

3. 2,199 + 5,832 =

    a. 8,331
    b. 8,041
    c. 8,141
    d. 8,031

4. 8,390 - 5,239 =

    a. 3,261
    b. 3,151
    c. 3,161
    d. 3,101

5. 643 - 587 =

    a. 56
    b. 66
    c. 46
    d. 55

6. 3,406 - 2,767 =

    a. 629
    b. 720
    c. 639
    d. 649

7. 149 × 7 =

    a. 1032
    b. 1043
    c. 1059
    d. 1063

8. 467 × 41 =

    a. 19,147
    b. 21,227
    c. 23,107
    d. 18,177

9. 309 × 17 =

    a. 5,303
    b. 4,913
    c. 4,773
    d. 5,253

10. 491 ÷ 9 =

    a. 54 r5

    b. 56 r6

    c. 57 r5

    d. 51 r

Decimals, Fractions and Percent

11. 15 is what percent of 200?

    a. 7.5%

    b. 15%

    c. 20%

    d. 17.50%

12. A boy has 5 red balls, 3 white balls and 2 yellow balls. What percent of the balls are yellow?

    a. 2%

    b. 8%

    c. 20%

    d. 12%

13. Add 10% of 300 to 50% of 20

    a. 50%

    b. 40%

    c. 60%

    d. 45%

14. Convert 75% to a fraction.

   a. 2/100
   b. 75/100
   c. 3/4
   d. 4/7

15. Convert 90% to a fraction

   a. 1/10
   b. 9/9
   c. 10/100
   d. 9/10

16. Multiply 3 by 25% of 40

   a. 75
   b. 30
   c. 68
   d. 35

17. What is 10% of 30 multiplied by 75% of 200?

   a. 450
   b. 750
   c. 20
   d. 45

18. Convert 0.28 to a fraction.

   a. 7/25
   b. 3.25
   c. 8/25
   d. 5/28

19. **Convert 0.45 to a fraction**

    a. 7/20
    b. 7/45
    c. 9/20
    d. 3/20

20. **Convert 1/5 to percent.**

    a. 10%
    b. 5%
    c. 20%
    d. 25%

21. **Convert 4/20 to percent**

    a. 25%
    b. 20%
    c. 40%
    d. 30%

22. **Convert 0.55 to percent**

    a. 45%
    b. 15%
    c. 75%
    d. 55%

23. **Convert 0.33 to percent**

    a. 77%
    b. 67%
    c. 33%
    d. 57%

24. A man buys an item for $420 and has a balance of $3000.00. How much did he have before?

    a. $2,580
    b. $3,420
    c. $2,420
    d. $342

25. Divide 9.60 by 3.2

    a. 2.50
    b. 3
    c. 2.3
    d. 6.4

26. What is the best approximate solution for 1.135 - 113.5?

    a. -110
    b. 100
    c. -90
    d. 110

Basic Algebra

27. If X = 7 solve 3x + 5 – 2x

    a. x = 6
    b. x = 12
    c. x = 1
    d. x = 0

28. Solve the following equation $3(2x - 2) = 24 - 3x$

    a. x = 24
    b. x = 9
    c. x = 10
    d. x = 3.33

29. Solve $3x - 27 = 0$

    a. x = 24
    b. x = 30
    c. x = 9
    d. x = 21

30. Solve the following equation $4(y + 6) = 3y + 30$

    a. y = 6
    b. y = 20
    c. y = 30/7
    d. y = 30

31. Expand $(x + 7)(x - 3)$

    a. $x^2 + 4x - 21$
    b. x + 21
    c. 2x + 4 - 21
    d. 6x - 21 2x + 4x - 21

Exponents

32. Express in 3^4 standard form

    a. 81
    b. 27
    c. 12
    d. 9

33. Simplify $4^3 + 2^4$

    a. 45
    b. 108
    c. 80
    d. 48

34. If x = 2 and y = 5, solve $xy^3 - x^3$

    a. 240
    b. 258
    c. 248
    d. 242

35. $X^3 \times X^2 =$

    a. 5^x
    b. x^{-5}
    c. x^{-1}
    d. X^5

36. Express 100000^0 in standard form.

    a. 1
    b. 0
    c. 100000
    d. 1000

37. Solve $\sqrt{144}$

    a. 14
    b. 72
    c. 24
    d. 12

38. What is the square root of √225 ?

a. 25
b. 15
c. 5
d. 13

39. What number is the largest?

5 % of 400
25% of 4000
2 % of 500
8% of 1000

40. What is the smallest value?

4 % of 4
5 % of 5
0.3% of 12
1/5 of 100

Answer Key

1. C
389 + 454 = 843

2. C
9,177 + 7,204 = 16,381

3. D
2,199 + 5,832 = 8,031

4. B
8,390 - 5,239 = 3,151

5. A
643 - 587 = 56

6. C
3,406 - 2,767 = 639

7. B
149 × 7 = 1043

8. A
467 × 41 = 19,147

9. D
309 × 17 = 52,53

10. A
491 ÷ 9 = 54 r5

Decimals, Percent and Fractions

11. A
15% = 15/100 X 200 = 7.5%

12. C
Total no. of balls = 10, no. of yellow balls = 2. 2/10 X 100 = 20%

13. B
10% of 300 = 30 and 50% of 20 = 10 so 30 + 10 = 40.

14. C
75%= 75/100 = ¾

15. D
90% = 90/100 = 9/10

16. B
25% of 40 = 10 and 10 x 3 = 30

17. A
10% of 30 = 3 and 75% of 200 = 150, 3 X 150 = 450

18. A
0.28 = 28/100 = 7/25

19. C
0.45 = 45/100 = 9/20

20. C
1/5 X 100 = 20%

21. B
4/20 X 100 = 1/5 X 100 = 20%

22. D
0.55 X 100 = 55%

23. C
0.33 X 100 = 33%

24. B
(Amount Spent) $420 + $3000 (Balance) = $3420

25. B
9.60/3.2 = 3

26. A
1.135 -113.5 = 1.135 -113.5 = -112.37. Best approximate = -110

Basic Algebra

27. B
X=7, so 3x = 3 x 7 = 21, 2x = 2 x 7 = 14, so 21 + 5 - 14 = 26 - 14 = 12

28. D
6x – 6 = 24 – 3x, 6x + 3x -6 = 24, = 9x – 6 = 24, = 9x = 24 + 6, = 9x = 30, = x = 30/9, = x = 3.33

29. C
3x = 27, x = 27/3, x = 9
4. B 4y + 6 = 3y + 30, = 4y – 3y + 6 = 30, = y + 6 = 30, = y = 30 – 6, = y = 24

30. A
4y + 24 = 3y + 30, = 4y – 3y + 24 = 30, = y + 24 = 30, = y = 30 – 24, = y = 6

31. A
Multiply the first bracket and the second. $x^2 - 3x + 7x - 21 = x^2 + 4x - 21$

Exponents

32. A
3 x 3 x 3 x 3 = 81

33. C
(4 x 4 x 4) + (2 x 2 x 2 x 2) = 64 + 16 = 80

34. D
$2(5)^3 - (2)^3$ = 2(125) – 8 = 250 – 8 = 242

35. D
$X^3 \times X^2 = X^{3+2} = X^5$
To multiply exponents with like bases, add the exponents.

36. A
Any value (except 0) raised to the power of 0 equals 1.

37. D
√144 = 12

38. B
√225 = 15.

39. B
a. 5% of 400 = 20
b. 25% of 4000 = 1000
c. 2% of 500 = 10
d. 8% of 1000 = 80

D is the largest.

40. C
a. 4% of 4 = .16
b. 5% of 5 = 0.25
c. 0.3% of 12 = 0.036
d. 1/5 of 100 = 20

C is the smallest.

Basic math Video Tutorials

https://www.test-preparation.ca/math-videos/

Fraction Tips, Tricks and Short-cuts

When you are writing an exam, time is precious, so anything you can do to answer questions faster is a real advantage.

Here are some ideas, Short-cuts, tips and tricks that can speed up answering fraction problems.

Remember that a fraction is just a number which names a portion of something. For instance, instead of having a whole pie, a fraction says you have a part of a pie--such as a half of one or a fourth of one.

Two numbers make up a fraction. The number on top is the numerator. The number on the bottom is the denominator.

To remember which is which, just remember that "denominator" and "down" both start with a "d." And the "downstairs" number is the denominator. So for instance, in ½, the numerator is 1, and the denominator (or "downstairs") number is 2.

Adding Fractions

It's easy to add two fractions if they have the same denominator. Just add the digits on top and leave the bottom one the same: 1/10 + 6/10 = 7/10.

It's the same with subtracting fractions with the same denominator: 7/10 - 6/10 = 1/10.

Adding and subtracting fractions with different denominators is a little more complicated.

First, you have to arrange the fractions so they have the same denominators.

The easiest way to do this is to multiply the denominators: For 2/5 + 1/2 multiply 5 by 2. Now you have a denominator of 10.

But now you have to change the top numbers too. Since you multiplied the 5 in 2/5 by 2, you also multiply the 2 by 2, to get 4. So the first fraction is now 4/10.

In the second fraction, you multiplied the denominator by 5, you have to multiply the numerator by 5 also, to get 5/10.

Now you have 4/10 + 5/10 and you can add 5 and 4 to get 9/10.

Simplest Form

To reduce a fraction to its simplest form, you have to arrange the numerator and denominator so the only common factor is 1.

Think of it this way:

Let's take an example: The fraction 2/10.

This is not reduced to its simplest terms because there is a number that will divide evenly into both: 2. We want to make it so that the only number that will divide evenly into both is 1.

Divide the top and bottom by 2 to get the new, reduced fraction - 1/5.

Multiplying Fractions

This is the easiest of all: Just multiply the two top numbers and then multiply the two bottom numbers.

Here is an example,

2/5 X 2/3

First, multiply the numerators: 2 X 2 = 4

then multiply the denominators: 5 X 3 = 15

Your answer is 4/15.

Dividing Fractions

Dividing fractions is easy if you remember a simple trick - first turn the second fraction upside down - then multiply!

Here is an example:

7/8 X 1/2

Turn the second fraction upside down:

7/8 X 2/1

then multiply:

(7 X 2) / (8 X 1) = 14/8

Converting Fractions to Decimals

There are a couple of ways to convert fractions to decimals. The first, which is the fastest -- is to memorize some basic fraction facts.

    1/100 is "one hundredth," expressed as a decimal, it's .01.

    1/50 is "two hundredths," expressed as a decimal, it's .02.

    1/25 is "one twenty-fifth" or "four hundredths," expressed as a decimal, it's .04.

1/20 is "one twentieth" or ""five hundredths," expressed as a decimal, it's .05.

1/10 is "one tenth," expressed as a decimal, it's .1.

1/8 is "one eighth," or "one hundred twenty-five thousandths," expressed as a decimal, it's .125.

1/5 is "one fifth," or "two tenths," expressed as a decimal, it's .2.

1/4 is "one fourth" or "twenty-five hundredths," expressed as a decimal, it's .25.

1/3 is "one third" or "thirty-three hundredths," expressed as a decimal, it's .33.

1/2 is "one half" or "five tenths," expressed as a decimal, it's .5.

3/4 is "three fourths," or "seventy-five hundredths," expressed as a decimal, it's .75.

Of course, if you're no good at memorization, another good technique for converting a fraction to a decimal is to manipulate it so that the fraction's denominator is 10, 100, 1000, or some other power of 10.

Here's an example: We'll start with three quarters. What is the first number in the 4 "times table" that you can multiply and get a multiple of 10? Can you multiply 4 by something to get 10? No. Can you multiply it by something to get 100? Yes! 4 X 25 is 100.

So multiply the numerator by 25, which is 75 over 100

We know fractions are really a division problem, and we also know that dividing by 100, means we move the decimal 2 places to the left.

So, 75 over 100 = .75

Lets try another example - Convert one fifth to a decimal.

First find a power of 10 that 5 goes into evenly, which is 2.

Multiply the numerator and denominator by 2, which is

two tenths.

Dividing 2 by 10 means we move the decimal place 1 place to the left.

So 1/5 = 0.5

Converting Fractions to Percent

Here is a quick method to convert fraction to percent and a strategy for answering on a multiple choice test that will save you valuable exam time.

First, remember that a fraction is a division problem: you're dividing the bottom number into the top.

Taking an example, convert 2/3 into percent.

The first method is to multiple the numerator by 100 and divide. So,

(2 X 100) / 2 = 100/3 = 66.66

Add a % sign and you have the answer, 66.66%

https://youtu.be/T9qiEHzwJEU?si=ZF9qVNLEF6JnPgqm

If you're doing these conversions on a multiple-choice test, here's an idea that might be even easier and faster. Let's say you have a fraction of 1/8 and you're asked to convert to percent.

Since we know that "percent" means hundredths, ask yourself what number we can multiply 8 by to get 100. Since there is no number, ask what number gets us close to 100.

That number is 12: 8 X 12 = 96. So it gets us a little less than 100. Now, whatever you do to the denominator, you have to do to the numerator. Let's multiply 1 X 12 and we get 12. However, since 96 is a little less than 100, we know that our answer will be a little MORE than 12%.

Look at the choices and eliminate the obvious wrong choices. So if your possible answers on the multiple-choice test are these:

a) 8.5% b) 19% c) 12.5% d) 25%

then we know the answer is c) 12.5%, because it's a little MORE than the 12 we got in our math problem above.

Here all the choices except choice C 12.5% can be eliminated.

You don't have to know the exact correct answer, just enough to estimate, then eliminate the obviously wrong answers.

This was an easy example to demonstrate the strategy, but don't be fooled! You probably won't get such an easy question on your exam. By estimating your answer quickly, then eliminating obviously incorrect choices immediately, you save precious exam time.

Most Common Fraction Mistakes on a Test

1. Not simplifying fractions first. Always simplify fractions to the simples form before adding, subtracting or other operations.

2. Not understanding common denominators.

To add or subtract fractions, they must have the same denominator. For example, to add 1/2 and 3/4, a common denominator is needed. The common denominator 4, because 4 is a multiple of both 2 and 4.

So, you would convert 1/2 to 2/4 and add it to 3/4 to get 2/4 + 3/4 = 5/4

3. Errors with mixed numbers and converting to improper fractions or vice versa.

Referring to the problem above, 5/4 is an improper fraction, since 5 (the numerator) is larger than 4 (the denominator). This can be converted to a mixed number – 5/4 = 4/4 + 1/4, and we know 4/4 = 1

so – 1 + 1/4 = 1 1/4.

4. Errors with equivalent fractions and reducing to the simplest form.

Here is question – Does 2/4 = 1/2 ?   YES! we can reduce 2/4 by dividing the numerator (top) and the denominator (bottom) by 2. so 2/4 divided by 2/2 = 1/2.

5. Errors canceling common factors in fractions.

Cancelling out common factors works like this – 2/4 X 4/8 These are divisible by 2 so we divide by 2 in the top of one side and bottom of the other – 1/4 X 4/4

We can do the same again with the bottom of the first fraction and the top of the second – 1/1 X 1/4   and since 1/1 = 1 we have 1 X 1/4 = 1/4.

6. Errors with basic arithmetic operations (addition, subtraction, multiplication, and division) with fractions.

Decimal Tips, Tricks and Shortcuts

Converting Decimals to Fractions

Converting decimals to fractions is easy if you say it the right way! If you say "point one" or "point 25," you'll have trouble.

But if you say, "one tenth" and "twenty-five hundredths," then you have already solved it! That's because, if you know your fractions, you know that "one tenth" looks like this: 1/10. And "twenty-five hundredths" looks like this: 25/100.

Even if you have digits before the decimal, such as 3.4, learning how to say the word will help you with the conversion into a fraction. It's not "three point four," it's "three and four tenths." Knowing this, you know that the fraction which looks like "three and four tenths" is 3 4/10.

The conversion is not complete until you reduce the fraction to its lowest terms: It's not 25/100, but 1/4.

Converting Decimals to Percent

Changing a decimal to a percent is easy if you remember one thing: multiply by 100.

For example, if you start with .45, simply multiply it by 100 for 45. Then add the % sign to the end - 45%.

Think of it this way: take out the decimal point, add a percent sign on the opposite side. In other words, the decimal on the left is replaced by the % on the right.

It doesn't work quite that easily if the decimal is in the middle of the number. For example, 3.7. Here, take out the decimal in the middle and replace it with a 0 % at the end. So 3.7 converted to decimal is 370%.

Percent Tips, Tricks and Short-cuts

Percent problems are not nearly as scary as they appear, if you remember this neat trick:

Draw a cross as in:

Portion	Percent
Whole	100

In the upper left, write PORTION. In the bottom left write WHOLE. In the top right, write PERCENT and in the bottom right, write 100. Whatever your problem is, you will leave blank the unknown, and fill in the other four parts. For example, let's suppose your problem is: Find 10% of 50. Since we know the 10% part, we put 10 in the percent corner. Since the whole number in our problem is 50, we put that in the corner marked whole. You always put 100 underneath the percent, so we leave it as is, which leaves only the top left corner blank. This is where we'll put our answer. Now simply multiply the two corner numbers that are NOT 100. Here, it's 10 X 50. That gives us 500. Now divide this by the remaining corner, or 100, to get a final answer of 5. 5 is the number that goes in the upper-left corner, and is your final solution.

Another hint to remember: Percents are the same thing as hundredths in decimals. So .45 is the same as 45 hundredths or 45 percent.

Percent Tips and Tricks Video

https://youtu.be/T9qiEHzwJEU?si=Vvo_WY8sdTPhF8S7

Converting Percents to Decimals

Percents are just a type of decimal, so it should be no surprise that converting between the two is actually fairly simple. Here are a few tricks and Short-cuts to keep in mind:

- Remember that percent literally means "per 100" or "for every 100." So when you speak of 30% you're saying 30 for every 100 or the fraction 30/100. In basic math, you learned that fractions that have 10 or 100 as the denominator can easily be turned to a decimal. 30/100 is thirty hundredths, or expressed as a decimal, .30.
- Another way to look at it: To convert a percent to a decimal, simply divide the number by 100. So for instance, if the percent is 47%, divide 47 by 100. The result will be .47. Get rid of the % mark and you're done.

- Remember that the easiest way of dividing by 100 is by moving your decimal two spots to the left.

Converting Percents to Fractions

Converting percents to fractions is easy. After all, a percent is just a type of fraction; it tells you what part of 100 that you're talking about. Here are some simple ideas for making the conversion from a percent to a fraction:

- If the percent is a whole number -- say 34% -- then simply write a fraction with 100 as the denominator (the bottom number). Then put the percentage itself on top. So 34% becomes 34/100.
- Now reduce as you would reduce any percent. Here, by dividing 2 into 34 and 2 into 100, you get 17/50.
- If your percent is not a whole number -- say 3.4% --then convert it to a decimal expressed as hundredths. 3.4 is the same as 3.40 (or 3 and forty hundredths). Now ask yourself how you would express "three and forty hundredths" as a fraction. It would, of course, be 3 40/100. Reduce this and it becomes 3 2/5.

How to Answer Basic Math Multiple Choice

The time allowed on the math portion of a standardized test is typically so short that there's no room for error. You have to be fast and accurate.

Math strategy is very helpful, but nothing beats knowing your stuff! Make sure that you have learned all the important formulas that will be used.

If you don't know the formulas, strategy won't help you.

How to Answer Basic Math Questions - the Basics

First, read the problem, but not the answers.

Work through the problem first and come up with your own answers. Hopefully, you should find your answer among the choices.

If no answer matches the one you got, re-check your math, but this time, use a different method. In math, there are different ways to solve a problem.

Math Multiple Choice Strategy

The two strategies for working with basic math multiple choice are Estimation and Elimination.

Estimation is just as it sounds - try to estimate an approximate answer first. Then look at the choices.

Elimination is probably the most powerful strategy for answering multiple choice.
Eliminate obviously incorrect answers and narrowing the possible choices.

Here are a few basic math examples of how this works.

Solve 2/3 + 5/12

    a. 9/17

    b. 3/11

    c. 7/12

    d. 1 1/12

First estimate the answer. 2/3 is more than half and 5/12 is about half, so the answer is going to be very close to 1.

Next, Eliminate. Choice A is about 1/2 and can be eliminated, choice B is very small, less than 1/2 and can be eliminated. Choice C is close to 1/2 and can be eliminated. Leaving only choice D, which is just over 1.

Work through the solution, find a common denominator and add. The correct answer is 1 1/12, so Choice D is correct.

Let's look at another example:

Solve 4/5 – 2/3

    a. 2/2
    b. 2/13
    c. 1
    d. 2/15

First, quickly estimate the answer. 4/5 is very close to 1, and 2/3 more than half, so the answer is going to be less than 1/2.

Choice A can be eliminated right away, because it is 1. Choice C can be eliminated for the same reason.

Next, look at the denominators. Since 5 and 3 don't go into 13, choice B can be eliminated as well.

That leaves choice D. Checking the answer, the common denominator will be 15. So the answer is 2/15 and choice D is correct.

Toolbox Math

Order Of Operation

Some math calculations contain more than one set of operations. For example, a problem like 3 + (35 - 21) x 2 requires addition, subtraction and multiplication operations. The problem arises from the confusion of which of the operations to perform first. Starting with the wrong operation will give you the wrong answer. To solve this dilemma and to avoid confusion, the Order of Operation rules were set.

Order of operation is a set of mathematical rules designed to be used for calculations that require more than one arithmetic operation. For example, calculation problems that require two or more out of addition, subtraction, multiplication and division, would require that you follow the order of operation to solve.

The order of operation rules are quite simple as explained below.

Rule 1:   Start with calculations that are inside brackets or parentheses.
Rule 2:   Then, solve all multiplications and divisions, from left to right.
Rule 3:   Finally, solve all additions and subtractions, from left to right.

Example 1

Solve 16 + 5 x 8

Based on the rules above, we would have to start with the multiplication part of the question.
That will give: 16 + 40 = 56

Take note that if the rule was not followed and addition was done first, the answer gotten would be different and wrong.

16 + 5 x 8
21 x 8 = 168 (wrong answer)

Example 2

3 +(35 - 21) x 2

Based on the rules of the order of operation, we have to solve the problem in the bracket or parenthesis first. Then we do the multiplication, before doing the addition.

3 + (35 - 21) x 2

3 + (14) x 2
3 + 28
= 31

WORD POWER: UNLOCKING THE BIG IDEAS

Welcome to the Vocabulary section. Whether you're an avid reader or someone who prefers a podcast, this chapter is designed to help you navigate the specific way the CAAT tests your word knowledge.

Inside, you'll find a Self-Assessment and a Tutorial focused on general principles like synonyms, antonyms, and context clues. Think of the tutorial as a "tune-up" for your brain. If you find some of the words or concepts a bit foreign, don't worry—that's exactly why we're here. If it feels like a real struggle, it might be a sign to grab a dictionary and start a daily reading habit alongside this guide.

The Vocabulary Self-Assessment

We use this "pre-test" to help you:

>**Pinpoint the Gaps:** Do you know the words but struggle with how they're paired?

>**Tailor Your Study Time:** If you ace this, you can spend more time on math. If not, you know where to focus.

Get a "Feel" for the Exam: The CAAT can change its "look" from year to year—sometimes they swap questions, change the time limits, or shuffle how sections are combined. While we don't have a crystal ball, these 10 questions are designed to mirror the level and style of the exam. If you can handle these, you can handle whatever the CAAT throws at you.

Build Stamina: Every bit of practice makes you more comfortable when the real timer starts ticking.

Timing and Strategy

The CAAT is a fast-paced test. For this self-assessment, we've given you 10 questions. I recommend setting a timer for 10 minutes to get used to that "one minute per question" rhythm. However, if you're just starting out at the kitchen table, feel free to take your time. Learning the logic behind the answers is more important than the speed—at least for today.

Checking Your Score

Once you've finished the 15 questions, see how you stack up. Here's my honest take on what your score means:

Score	What it means...
75% – 100%	**Excellent.** You've got this down pat! You're ready to move forward.
50% – 75%	**Good.** You've got the basics, but there's room to sharpen the saw. I'd suggest a quick skim of the tutorials to pick up a few extra points.
25% – 50%	**Below Average.** You might be struggling with how the questions are framed. Take a beat, go through the tutorials carefully, and try the quiz again in a few days.
Under 25%	**Needs Work.** Don't get discouraged! It just means we need to build a stronger foundation. Spend some quality time with the tutorials before moving on to the full practice tests.

PASS THE CAAT!

Vocabulary Answer Sheet

Vocabulary – Unlocking Big Ideas

Vocabulary Self-Assessment

Choose the word that best suits the given definition.

1. Something that is corrupted or impure is
   a. Adulterate
   b. Harbor
   c. Infuriate
   d. Inculcate

2. Doing something eagerly is doing it with
   a. Alacrity
   b. Happiness
   c. Donator
   d. Marital

3. To make less severe is to
   a. Suspense
   b. Alleviate
   c. Ingrate
   d. Action

4. To make blissful or happy is to
   a. Brand
   b. Negate
   c. Beatify
   d. Train

5. One who gives a gift or who gives money to a charity organization is a

   a. Captain
   b. Benefactor
   c. Source
   d. Teacher

6. Something that is hidden, secret, or disguised, is

   a. Accustomed
   b. Covert
   c. Hide
   d. Carriage

7. Straightforward, open and sincere is

   a. Lawful
   b. Candid
   c. True
   d. Lawful

8. Fearless is the same as

   a. Feeble
   b. Strongest
   c. Dauntless
   d. Super

9. To remove a leader or high official from position is to

   a. Sack
   b. Suspend
   c. Depose
   d. Dropped

10. To build up or strengthen relative to morals or religion, is to

    a. Sanctify

    b. Amplify

    c. Edify

    d. Wry

Answer Key

1. A
Adulterate VERB corrupted; impure; adulterated.

2. A
Alacrity NOUN eagerness; liveliness; enthusiasm.

3. B
Alleviate VERB to make less severe, as a pain or difficulty.

4. C
Beatify VERB to make blissful.

5. B
Benefactor NOUN somebody who gives one a gift. Usually refers to someone who gives money to a charity or another form of organization.

6. B
Covert ADJECTIVE Partially hidden, disguised, secret, surreptitious.

7. B
Candid ADJECTIVE straightforward, open and sincere.

8. C
Dauntless ADJECTIVE invulnerable to fear or intimidation.

9. C
Depose VERB to remove (a leader) from (high) office, without killing the incumbent.

10. C
Edify VERB to instruct or improve morally or intellectually.

Vocabulary- Unlocking Big Ideas
Taming the Big Words: A Practical Guide

Let's be honest: looking at a dictionary when you're prepping for an exam is enough to make anyone's head spin. There are hundreds of thousands of words in the English language, and trying to memorize them all is a fool's errand.

The good news? You don't have to.

Instead of trying to "swallow the ocean," we're going to learn how to fish. Here are my favorite strategies for handling those "big words" without losing your cool.

1. Play Word Surgeon: Take Them Apart

Most big words are just a bunch of small parts glued together. We call these **Prefixes** (at the start), **Roots** (the heart), and **Suffixes** (at the end).

Take the root **"Ambi"** (which means "both").
- If you're **ambidextrous**, you're skilled with *both* hands.
- If a situation is **ambiguous**, it has *both* (or many) meanings.
- If you feel **ambivalent**, you have *both* good and bad feelings about something.

If you learn one root word, you've suddenly unlocked the door to five or six other words. It's a "two-for-one" deal that Big Prep won't tell you about.

2. Watch Out for "Double Agents"

Some words have more than one job. You probably know that a **"husband"** is a partner in a marriage. But did you know that to **"husband"** your resources means to be thrifty or careful with them?

Always look at the *context*. If a word seems out of place, it might be working its second job.

3. The "Slow and Steady" Method (Read!)

I'll say it straight: reading is the best vocabulary builder there is. When you see a word in a story or a news article, your brain remembers it better because it has a "home" (context). Now, if your exam is tomorrow, this won't help much. But if you have a few weeks, try to read something slightly

challenging for 15 minutes a day. It's the best long-term investment you can make.
4. Practical Tips for Fast Results

- **Make a Commitment:** Try to learn just two new words a day. By the end of the month, that's 60 new tools in your belt.
- **Use It or Lose It:** When you learn a new word, try to slip it into a conversation or a text message. Say it out loud when you're making coffee. The more you use it, the deeper it sticks.
- **Keep a Dictionary Handy:** Whether it's an old-school book or an app on your phone, look words up the moment you see them. If you can't do it right then, jot them down in a "New Words" notebook.
- **The Power of the Pen:** Speaking of notebooks—**write it down!** Printing a list off the internet isn't the same. There's a "magic connection" between the hand and the brain. When you physically write a word and its meaning, you're "imprinting" it on your memory. Hitting 'Print' doesn't do that.
- **Flashcards:** These are your best friend. Keep a small stack in your pocket. Whether you're waiting for the bus in Victoria or sitting in a waiting room, you can knock out five minutes of study.

5. Synonyms and Antonyms
Think of words as families. The word "big" has about 75 cousins (synonyms) like *massive, gargantuan,* or *immense.* It also has 75 "opposites" (antonyms) like *tiny, microscopic,* or *minuscule.* Learning these in groups gives your brain a framework to hang them on.

A Note on Word Order: Sometimes, the CAAT will throw a curveball with "inverse word order." This is just a fancy way of saying the sentence is flipped. Instead of saying "The dog ran," they might say "Down the street ran the dog." Don't let the structure trip you up—the meaning is still the same!

Putting It All Together - Practice Test 1

You've done the heavy lifting—reviewing the math, sharpening your vocabulary, and tackling those reading passages. Now it's time to see how all those pieces fit together.

I'll be honest with you: these aren't the exact questions you'll see on the CAAT. If I told you they were, I'd be pulling your leg! Nobody knows exactly what the examiners will dream up this year, and they're famous for swapping questions around or tweaking the format. But don't let that rattle you. We've designed these questions to mirror the "DNA" of the real exam. If you can navigate these waters, you'll be ready for whatever the CAAT throws at you.

How to Get the Most Out of This Test
To get a true sense of where you stand, you need to treat this like the real deal. No TV in the background, no checking your phone, and definitely no "peeking" at the answers halfway through!

> **Find Your "Quiet Corner":** Pick a time and place where you won't be disturbed. Whether it's the kitchen table early in the morning or a quiet desk at the library, make sure it's just you and the paper.

Follow the Rules: Read the instructions for each section carefully. The real CAAT is as much about following directions as it is about knowing the answers.

Use the Bubble Sheets: It might feel a bit "old school," but filling in those little circles is part of the test experience. We've provided sheets for you to use—don't just circle the answers in the book!

Review Your Work: Once you're finished, check your answers against the key. Don't just look at what you got wrong—read the explanations. Understanding why an answer is correct is where the real learning happens.

A Quick Word on Pacing

Don't try to be a hero and do multiple practice tests in one day. Your brain is a muscle, and it needs time to recover after a big workout.

After you finish this first test, take a breather. Spend two or three days reviewing the areas where you felt a bit shaky. Let the information "sink in" before you move on to the next set of questions.

You've got the tools. You've done the work. Now, take a deep breath and give it your best shot.

Reading Comprehension Answer Sheet

	A	B	C	D	E		A	B	C	D	E
1	○	○	○	○	○	21	○	○	○	○	○
2	○	○	○	○	○	22	○	○	○	○	○
3	○	○	○	○	○	23	○	○	○	○	○
4	○	○	○	○	○	24	○	○	○	○	○
5	○	○	○	○	○	25	○	○	○	○	○
6	○	○	○	○	○	26	○	○	○	○	○
7	○	○	○	○	○	27	○	○	○	○	○
8	○	○	○	○	○	28	○	○	○	○	○
9	○	○	○	○	○	29	○	○	○	○	○
10	○	○	○	○	○	30	○	○	○	○	○
11	○	○	○	○	○	31	○	○	○	○	○
12	○	○	○	○	○	32	○	○	○	○	○
13	○	○	○	○	○	33	○	○	○	○	○
14	○	○	○	○	○	34	○	○	○	○	○
15	○	○	○	○	○	35	○	○	○	○	○
16	○	○	○	○	○	36	○	○	○	○	○
17	○	○	○	○	○	37	○	○	○	○	○
18	○	○	○	○	○	38	○	○	○	○	○
19	○	○	○	○	○	39	○	○	○	○	○
20	○	○	○	○	○	40	○	○	○	○	○

Number Operations Answer Sheet

	A	B	C	D	E		A	B	C	D	E
1	○	○	○	○	○	21	○	○	○	○	○
2	○	○	○	○	○	22	○	○	○	○	○
3	○	○	○	○	○	23	○	○	○	○	○
4	○	○	○	○	○	24	○	○	○	○	○
5	○	○	○	○	○	25	○	○	○	○	○
6	○	○	○	○	○	26	○	○	○	○	○
7	○	○	○	○	○	27	○	○	○	○	○
8	○	○	○	○	○	28	○	○	○	○	○
9	○	○	○	○	○	29	○	○	○	○	○
10	○	○	○	○	○	30	○	○	○	○	○
11	○	○	○	○	○	31	○	○	○	○	○
12	○	○	○	○	○	32	○	○	○	○	○
13	○	○	○	○	○	33	○	○	○	○	○
14	○	○	○	○	○	34	○	○	○	○	○
15	○	○	○	○	○	35	○	○	○	○	○
16	○	○	○	○	○	36	○	○	○	○	○
17	○	○	○	○	○	37	○	○	○	○	○
18	○	○	○	○	○	38	○	○	○	○	○
19	○	○	○	○	○	39	○	○	○	○	○
20	○	○	○	○	○	40	○	○	○	○	○

Vocabulary Answer Sheet

	A	B	C	D	E		A	B	C	D	E
1	○	○	○	○	○	21	○	○	○	○	○
2	○	○	○	○	○	22	○	○	○	○	○
3	○	○	○	○	○	23	○	○	○	○	○
4	○	○	○	○	○	24	○	○	○	○	○
5	○	○	○	○	○	25	○	○	○	○	○
6	○	○	○	○	○	26	○	○	○	○	○
7	○	○	○	○	○	27	○	○	○	○	○
8	○	○	○	○	○	28	○	○	○	○	○
9	○	○	○	○	○	29	○	○	○	○	○
10	○	○	○	○	○	30	○	○	○	○	○
11	○	○	○	○	○						
12	○	○	○	○	○						
13	○	○	○	○	○						
14	○	○	○	○	○						
15	○	○	○	○	○						
16	○	○	○	○	○						
17	○	○	○	○	○						
18	○	○	○	○	○						
19	○	○	○	○	○						
20	○	○	○	○	○						

Part I - Reading Comprehension

Directions: The following questions are based on several reading passages. Each passage is followed by a series of questions. Read each passage carefully, and then answer the questions based on it. You may reread the passage as often as you wish. When you have finished answering the questions based on one passage, go right onto the next passage. Choose the best answer based on the information given and implied.

Questions 1 – 4 refer to the following passage.

Passage 1 - The Life of Helen Keller

Many people have heard of Helen Keller. She is famous because she was unable to see or hear, but learned to speak and read and went onto attend college and earn a degree. Her life is a very interesting story, one that she developed into an autobiography, which was then adapted into both a stage play and a movie. How did Helen Keller overcome her disabilities to become a famous woman? Read on to find out.
Helen Keller was not born blind and deaf. When she was a small baby, she had a very high fever for several days. As a result of her sudden illness, baby Helen lost her eyesight and her hearing. Because she was so young when she went deaf and blind, Helen Keller never had any recollection of being able to see or hear. Since she could not hear, she could not learn to talk. Since she could not see, it was difficult for her to move around. For the first six years of her life, her world was very still and dark.

Imagine what Helen's childhood was like. She could not hear her mother's voice. She could not see the beauty of her parent's farm. She could not recognize who was giving her a hug, or a bath or even where her bedroom was each night. Worse, she could not communicate with her parents in any way. She could not express her feelings or tell them the things she wanted. It must have been a very sad childhood.

When Helen was six years old, her parents hired her a teacher named Anne Sullivan. Anne was a young woman who was almost blind. However, she could hear and she could read Braille, so she was a perfect teacher for young Helen. At first, Anne had a very hard time teaching Helen anything. She described her first impression of Helen as a "wild thing, not a child." Helen did not like Anne at first either. She bit and hit Anne when Anne tried to teach her. However, the two of them eventually came to have a great deal of love and respect.

Anne taught Helen to hear by putting her hands on people's throats. She could feel the sounds people made. In time, Helen learned to feel what people said. Next, Anne taught Helen to read Braille, which is a way that books are written for the blind. Finally, Anne taught Helen to talk. Although Helen did learn to talk, it was hard for anyone but Anne to understand her.

As Helen grew older, she amazed more and more people with her story. She went to college and wrote books about her life. She gave talks to the public, with Anne at her side, translating her words. Today, both Anne Sullivan and Helen Keller are famous women who are respected for their lives' work.

1. Helen Keller could not see and hear and so, what was her biggest problem in childhood?

    a. Inability to communicate

    b. Inability to walk

    c. Inability to play

    d. Inability to eat

2. Helen learned to hear by feeling the vibrations people made when they spoke. What were these vibrations were felt through?

    a. Mouth

    b. Throat

    c. Ears

    d. Lips

3. From the passage, we can infer that Anne Sullivan was a patient teacher. We can infer this because

    a. Helen hit and bit her and Anne remained her teacher.

    b. Anne taught Helen to read only.

    c. Anne was hard of hearing too.

    d. Anne wanted to be a teacher.

4. Helen Keller learned to speak but Anne translated her words when she spoke in public. The reason Helen needed a translator was because

    a. Helen spoke another language.

    b. Helen's words were hard for people to understand.

    c. Helen spoke very quietly.

    d. Helen did not speak but only used sign language.

Questions 5 – 7 refer to the following passage.

Passage 2 - Ways Characters Communicate in Theater

Playwrights give their characters voices in a way that gives depth and added meaning to what happens on stage during their play. There are different types of speech in scripts that allow characters to talk with themselves, with other characters, and even with the audience.

It is very unique to theater that characters may talk "to themselves." When characters do this, the speech they give is called a soliloquy. Soliloquies are usually poetic, introspective, moving, and can tell audience members about the feelings, motivations, or suspicions of an individual character without that character having to reveal them to other characters on stage. "To be or not to be" is a famous soliloquy given by Hamlet as he considers difficult but important themes, such as life and death.

The most common type of communication in plays is when one character is speaking to another or a group of other characters. This is generally called dialogue, but can also be called monologue if one character speaks without being interrupted for a long time. It is not necessarily the most important type of communication, but it is the most common because the plot of the play cannot really progress without it. Lastly, and most unique to theater (although it has been used somewhat in film) is when a character speaks directly to the audience. This is called an aside, and scripts usually specifically direct actors to do this. Asides are usually comical, an inside joke between the character and the audience, and very short. The actor will usually face the audience when delivering them, even if it's for a moment, so the audience can recognize this move as an aside.

All three of these types of communication are important to the art of theater, and have been perfected by famous playwrights like Shakespeare. Understanding these types of communication can help an audience member grasp what is artful about the script and action of a play.

5. According to the passage, characters in plays communicate to

    a. move the plot forward

    b. show the private thoughts and feelings of one character

    c. make the audience laugh

    d. add beauty and artistry to the play

6. When Hamlet delivers "To be or not to be," he can be described as

    a. solitary

    b. thoughtful

    c. dramatic

    d. hopeless

7. The author uses parentheses to punctuate "although it has been used somewhat in film,"

    a. to show that films are less important

    b. instead of using commas so that the sentence is not interrupted

    c. because parenthesis help separate details that are not as important

    d. to show that films are not as artistic

Questions 8 – 11 refer to the following passage.

Passage 3 - Low Blood Sugar

As the name suggest, low blood sugar is low sugar levels in the bloodstream. This can occur when you have not eaten properly and undertake strenuous activity, or, when you are very hungry. When Low blood sugar occurs regularly and is ongoing, it is a medical condition called hypoglycaemia. This condition can occur in diabetics and in healthy adults.

Causes of low blood sugar can include excessive alcohol consumption, metabolic problems, stomach surgery, pancreas, liver or kidneys problems, as well as a side-effect of some medications.

Symptoms

There are different symptoms depending on the severity of the case.

Mild hypoglycaemia can lead to feelings of nausea and hunger. The patient may also feel nervous, jittery and have fast heart beats. Sweaty skin, clammy and cold skin are likely symptoms.

Moderate hypoglycaemia can result in a short temper, confusion, nervousness, fear and blurring of vision. The patient may feel weak and unsteady.

Severe cases of hypoglycaemia can lead to seizures, coma, fainting spells, nightmares, headaches, excessive sweats and severe tiredness.

Diagnosis of low blood sugar

A doctor can diagnosis this medical condition by asking the patient questions and testing blood and urine samples. Home testing kits are available for patients to monitor blood sugar levels. It is important to see a qualified doctor though. A doctor can test to safely rule out other medical conditions that could affect blood sugar levels.

Treatment

Quick treatments include drinking or eating foods and drinks with high sugar contents. Good examples include soda, fruit juice, hard candy and raisins. Glucose energy tablets can also help. Doctors may also recommend medications and well as changes in diet and exercise routine to treat chronic low blood sugar.

8. Based on the article, which of the following is true?

   a. Low blood sugar can happen to anyone.

   b. Low blood sugar only happens to diabetics.

   c. Low blood sugar can occur even.

   d. None of the statements are true.

9. Which of the following are the author's opinion?

   a. Quick treatments include drinking or eating foods and drinks with high sugar contents.

   b. None of the statements are opinions.

   c. This condition can occur in diabetics and in healthy adults.

   d. There are different symptoms depending on the severity of the case

10. What is the author's purpose?

   a. To inform

   b. To persuade

   c. To entertain

   d. To analyze

11. Which of the following is not a detail?

   a. A doctor can diagnosis this medical condition by asking the patient questions and testing.

   b. A doctor will test blood and urine samples.

   c. Glucose energy tablets can also help.

   d. Home test kits monitor blood sugar levels.

Questions 12 – 15 refer to the following passage.

How To Get A Good Nights Sleep

Sleep is just as essential for healthy living as water, air and food. Sleep allows the body to rest and replenish depleted energy levels. Sometimes we may for various reasons have trouble sleeping which has a serious effect on our health. Those who have prolonged sleeping problems are facing a serious medical condition and should see a qualified doctor when possible for help. Here is simple guide that can help you sleep better at night.

Try to create a natural pattern of waking up and sleeping around the same time every day - avoid going to bed too early and sleeping past your usual wake up time. Going to bed and getting up at radically different times everyday confuses your body clock. Try to establish a natural rhythm as much as you can.

Exercises and a bit of physical activity can help you sleep better at night. If you are having problem sleeping, try to be as active as you can during the day. If you are tired from physical activity, falling asleep is a natural and easy process for your body. If you remain inactive during the day, you will find it harder to sleep properly at night. Try walking, jogging, swimming or simple stretches close to your bed time.

Afternoon naps are great to refresh you during the day, but they may also keep you awake at night. If you feel sleepy during the day, get up, take a walk and get busy to keep from sleeping. Stretching is a good way to increase blood flow to the brain and keep you alert so that you don't sleep during the day. This will help you sleep better night.

> A warm bath or a glass of milk in the evening can help your body relax and prepare for sleep. A cold bath will wake you up and keep you up for several hours. Also avoid eating too late before bed.

12. How would you describe this sentence?

    a. A recommendation

    b. An opinion

    c. A fact

    d. A diagnosis

13. Which of the following is an alternative title for this article?

    a. Exercise and a good night's sleep

    b. Benefits of a good night's sleep

    c. Tips for a good night's sleep

    d. Lack of sleep is a serious medical condition

14. Which of the following cannot be inferred from this article?

    a. Biking is helpful for getting a good night's sleep

    b. Mental activity is helpful for getting a good night's sleep

    c. Eating bedtime snacks is not recommended

    d. Getting up at the same time is helpful for a good night's sleep

15. What is a disadvantage of taking naps?

    a. They may keep you awake.

    b. There are no disadvantages

    c. They may help you sleep better

    d. They may affect your diet

Questions 16 – 19 refer to the following passage.

Passage 5 - Pearl Harbour

In 1941, the world was at war. The United States was trying to stay out of the conflict. In Europe, the countries of Germany and Italy had formed an alliance to expand their land and territory. Germany had already taken over Poland, Denmark, and parts of France. They were heading next toward England and due to all the fighting in Europe, there were battles taking place as far south as North Africa, where the German and Italian armies were fighting the British.

This got even worse when the Asian nation of Japan formed an alliance with Germany and Italy. Together, the three countries called themselves, the AXIS. Now, the war was in the Pacific as well as in Europe and Northern Africa. Many Americans thought that perhaps now was the time for the United States to join with its ally, Great Britain and stop the Axis from taking over more regions of the world.
In 1941, Franklin Roosevelt was President of the United

States. His fear at the time was that Japan would try to take over many countries in Asia. He did not want to see that happen, so he moved some of the United States warships that had been stationed in San Diego, to the military base at Pearl Harbor, in Honolulu, Hawaii.

Japan quietly plotted their attack. They waited until the early hours of the morning on Sunday, December 7, 1941. Then, 350 Japanese war plans began to drop bombs on the U.S. ships at Pearl Harbor. The first bombs fell at 7:48 a.m. and only 90 minutes later, the attack was over. Pearl Harbor was decimated. 8 battleships were damaged. Eleven ships were sunk and 300 U.S. planes were destroyed. Most devastating was the loss of life 2,400 U.S. military members was killed in the attack and 1, 282 were injured.

President Roosevelt addressed the country via the radio and said "Today is a day that will live in infamy." He asked Congress to declare war on Japan. War was declared on Japan on December 8th and on Germany and Italy on December 11th. The United States had entered World War Two.

16. After reading the passage, what can you infer infamy means?

    a. Famous

    b. Remembered in a good way

    c. Remembered in a bad way

    d. Easily forgotten

17. What three countries formed the Axis?

    a. Italy, England, Germany

    b. United States, England, Italy

    c. Germany, Japan, Italy

    d. Germany, Japan, United States

18. What do you think was President Roosevelt's reason for moving warships to Pearl Harbour?

    a. He feared Japan would bomb San Diego

    b. He knew Japan was going to attack Pearl Harbor

    c. He was planning to attack Japan

    d. He wanted to try to protect Asian countries from Japanese takeover

19. Why do you think Japan chose a Sunday morning at 7:48 am for their attack?

    a. They knew the military slept late

    b. There is a law against bombing countries on a Sunday

    c. They wanted the attack to catch people by surprise

    d. That was the only free time they had to attack.

Questions 20 - 23 refer to the following recipe.

If You Have Allergies, You're Not Alone

People who experience allergies might joke that their immune systems have let them down or are seriously lacking. Truthfully though, people who experience allergic reactions or allergy symptoms during certain times of the year have heightened immune systems that are, "better" than those of people who have perfectly healthy but less militant immune systems.

Still, when a person has an allergic reaction, they are having an adverse reaction to a substance that is considered normal to most people. Mild allergic reactions usually have symptoms like itching, runny nose, red eyes, or bumps or discoloration of the skin. More serious allergic reactions, such as those to animal and insect poisons or certain foods, may result in the closing of the throat, swelling of the eyes, low blood pressure, inability to breath, and can even be fatal.

Different treatments help different allergies, depending on the nature and severity of the allergy. It is recommended to patients with severe allergies to take extra precautions, such as carrying an EpiPen, which treats anaphylactic shock and may prevent death, always in order for the remedy to be readily available and more effective. When an allergy is not so severe, treatments may be used just relieve a person of uncomfortable symptoms. Over the counter allergy medicines treat milder symptoms, and can be bought at any grocery store and used in moderation to help people with allergies live normally.

There are many tests available to assess whether a person has allergies or what they may be allergic to, and advances in these tests and the medicine used to treat patients continues to improve. Despite this fact, allergies still affect many people throughout the year or even every day. Medicines used to treat allergies have side-effects, and it is difficult to bring the body into balance with the use of medicine. Regardless, many of those who live with allergies are grateful for what is available and find it useful in maintaining their lifestyles.

20. According to this passage, which group does the word "militant" belong in

    a. sickly, ailing, faint

    b. strength, power, vigour

    c. active, fighting, warring

    d. worn, tired, breaking down

21. The author says that "medicines used to treat allergies have side-effects of their own" to

    a. point out that doctors aren't very good at diagnosing and treating allergies

    b. argue that because of the large number of people with allergies, a cure will never be found

    c. explain that allergy medicines aren't cures, and some compromise must be made

    d. argue that more wholesome remedies should be researched and medicines banned

22. It can be inferred that _____ recommend that some people with allergies carry medicine with them.

    a. the author

    b. doctors

    c. the makers of EpiPen

    d. people with allergies

23. The author has written this passage to

    a. inform readers on symptoms of allergies so people with allergies can get help

    b. persuade readers to be proud of having allergies

    c. inform readers on different remedies so people with allergies receive the right help

    d. describe different types of allergies, their symptoms, and their remedies

Questions 24 – 25 refer to the following email.

SUBJECT: MEDICAL STAFF CHANGES

To all staff:

This email is to advise you of a paper on recommended medical staff changes has been posted to the Human Resources website.

The contents are of primary interest to medical staff, other staff may be interested in reading it, particularly those in medical support roles.

The paper deals with several major issues:

1. Improving our ability to attract top quality staff to the hospital, and retain our existing staff. These changes will make our position and departmental names internationally recognizable and comparable with North American and North Asian departments and positions.

2. Improving our ability to attract top quality staff by introducing greater flexibility in the departmental structure.

3. General comments on issues to be further discussed relative to research staff.

The changes outlined in this paper are significant. I encourage you to read the document and send to me any comments you may have, so that it can be enhanced and improved.

Gordon Simms
Administrator,
Seven Oaks Regional Hospital

24. Are all hospital staff required to read the document posted to the Human Resources website?

    a. Yes all staff are required to read the document.
    b. No, reading the document is optional.
    c. Only medical staff are required to read the document.
    d. none of the above are correct.

25. Have the changes to medical staff been made?

    a. Yes, the changes have been made.
    b. No, the changes are only being discussed.
    c. Some of the changes have been made.
    d. None of the choices are correct.

Questions 26 – 29 refer to the following passage.

When a Poet Longs to Mourn, He Writes an Elegy

Poems are an expressive, especially emotional, form of writing. They have been in literature virtually from the time civilizations invented the written word. Poets often portrayed as moody, secluded, and even troubled, but this is because poets are introspective and feel deeply about the current events and cultural norms they are surrounded with. Poets often produce the most telling literature, giving insight into the society and mind-set they come from. This can be done in many forms.

The oldest types of poems often include many stanzas, which may or may not rhyme, and are more about telling a story than experimenting with language or words. The most common types of ancient poetry are epics, which are usually extremely long stories that follow a hero through his journey, or ellegies, which are often solemn in tone and used to mourn or lament something or someone. The Mesopotamians are often said to have invented the written word, and their literature is among the oldest in the world, including the epic poem titled "Epic of Gilgamesh." Similar in style and length to "Gilgamesh" is "Beowulf," an ellegy written in Old English and set in Scandinavia. These poems are often used by professors as the earliest examples of literature.

The importance of poetry was revived in the Renaissance. At this time, Europeans discovered the style and beauty of ancient Greek arts, and poetry was among those. Shakespeare is the most well-known poet of the time, and he used poetry not only to write poems but also to write plays for the theater. The most popular forms of poetry during the Renaissance included villanelles, (a nineteen-line poetic form) sonnets, as well as the epic. Poets during this time focused on style and form, and developed very specific rules and outlines for how an exceptional poem should be written.

As often happens in the arts, modern poets have rejected the constricting rules of Renaissance poets, and free form poems are much more popular. Some modern poems would read just like stories if they weren't arranged into lines and stanzas. It is difficult to tell which poems and poets will be the most important, because works of art often become more famous in hindsight, after the poet has died and society can look at itself without being in the moment. Modern poetry continues to develop, and will no doubt continue to change as values, thought, and writing continue to change.

Poems can be among the most enlightening and uplifting texts for a person to read if they are looking to connect with the past, connect with other people, or try to gain an understanding of what is happening in their time.

26. In summary, the author has written this passage

    a. as a foreword that will introduce a poem in a book or magazine

    b. because she loves poetry and wants more people to like it

    c. to give a brief history of poems

    d. to convince students to write poems

27. The author organizes the paragraphs mainly by

    a. moving chronologically, explaining which types of poetry were common in that time

    b. talking about new types of poems each paragraph and explaining them a little

    c. focusing on one poet or group of people and the poems they wrote

    d. explaining older types of poetry so she can talk about modern poetry

28. The author's claim that poetry has been around "virtually from the time civilizations invented the written word" is supported by the detail that

    a. Beowulf is written in Old English, which is not really in use any longer

    b. epic poems told stories about heroes

    c. the Renaissance poets tried to copy Greek poets

    d. the Mesopotamians are credited with both inventing the word and writing "Epic of Gilgamesh"

29. According to the passage, the word "telling" means

    a. speaking

    b. significant

    c. soothing

    d. wordy

Questions 30 refers to the following passage.

Scottish Wind Farms

The Scottish Government has a targeted plan of generating 100% of Scotland's electricity through renewable energy by 2020. Renewable energy sources include solar, water and wind power. Scotland uses all forms but its fastest growing energy is wind energy. Onshore and offshore wind turbines generate wind power. Wind turbines that are grouped together in large numbers are called wind farms. Most Scottish citizens say that the wind farms are necessary to meet current and future energy needs, and would like to see an increase in the number of wind farms.

They cite the fact that wind energy does not cause pollution, there are low operational costs, and most importantly, by definition, renewable energy it cannot be depleted.

30. What is Scotland's fastest growing source of renewable energy?

    a. Solar Panels
    b. Hydroelectric
    c. Wind
    d. Fossil Fuels

Part II – Number Operations

1. What is 1/3 of 3/4?

    a. 1/4
    b. 1/3
    c. 2/3
    d. 3/4

2. What fraction of $75 is $1500?

    a. 1/14
    b. 3/5
    c. 7/10
    d. 1/20

3. 3.14 + 2.73 + 23.7 =

    a. 28.57
    b. 30.57
    c. 29.56
    d. 29.57

4. A woman spent 15% of her income on an item and ends with $120. What percentage of her income is left?

    a. 12%
    b. 85%
    c. 75%
    d. 95%

5. Express 0.27 + 0.33 as a fraction.

    a. 3/6
    b. 4/7
    c. 3/5
    d. 2/7

6. What is (3.13 + 7.87) X 5?

    a. 65
    b. 50
    c. 45
    d. 55

7. Reduce 2/4 X 3/4 to lowest terms.

    a. 6/12
    b. 3/8
    c. 6/16
    d. 3/4

8. 2/3 − 2/5 =

    a. 4/10
    b. 1/15
    c. 3/7
    d. 4/15

9. 2/7 + 2/3 =

   a. 12/23
   b. 5/10
   c. 20/21
   d. 6/21

10. 2/3 of 60 + 1/5 of 75 =

    a. 45
    b. 55
    c. 15
    d. 50

11. 8 is what percent of 40?

    a. 10%
    b. 15%
    c. 20%
    d. 25%

12. 9 is what percent of 36?

    a. 10%
    b. 15%
    c. 20%
    d. 25%

13. Three tenths of 90 equals:

    a. 18
    b. 45
    c. 27
    d. 36

14. .4% of 36 is

    a. 1.44
    b. .144
    c. 14.4
    d. 144

15. If y = 4 and x = 3, solve yx^3

    a. -108
    b. 108
    c. 27
    d. 4

16. 5x + 3 = 7x -1. Find x

    a. 1/3
    b. ½
    c. 1
    d. 2

17. 5x + 2(x + 7) = 14x – 7. Find x

    a. 1
    b. 2
    c. 3
    d. 4

18. 12t -10 = 14t + 2. Find t

    a. -6
    b. -4
    c. 4
    d. 6

19. 5(z + 1) = 3(z + 2) + 11. Z=?

   a. 2
   b. 4
   c. 6
   d. 12

20. The price of a book went up from $20 to $25. What percent did the price increase?

   a. 5%
   b. 10%
   c. 20%
   d. 25%

21. The price of a book decreased from $25 to $20. What percent did the price decrease?

   a. 5%
   b. 10%
   c. 20%
   d. 25%

22. Mr. Brown bought 5 cheese burgers, 3 drinks, and 4 fries for his family, and a cookie pack for his dog. If the price of all single items is the same at $1.30 and a 3.5% tax is added, what is the total cost of dinner for Mr. Brown?

   a. $16
   b. $16.9
   c. $17
   d. $17.5

23. How much pay does Mr. Johnson receive if he gives half of his pay to his family, $250 to his landlord, and has exactly 3/7 of his pay left over?

    a. $3600
    b. $3500
    c. $2800
    d. $1750

24. A store sells a tool for $545. If a 15% value added tax is added to the price as, what is the actual cost of the tool?

    a. $490.40
    b. $473.90
    c. $505.00
    d. $503.15

25. The price of a product was hiked up by 45%. If the initial cost of the product was $220, what is the new cost of the product?

    a. $230
    b. $300
    c. $319
    d. $245

26. A worker's weekly salary was increased by 30%. If his new salary is $150, what was his old salary?

    a. $120
    b. $99.15
    c. $109
    d. $115.4

27. What is the difference between 700,653 and 70,099?

   a. 4,607,854
   b. 5,460
   c. 700,765
   d. 630,554

28. Simplify 0.12 + 1 2/5 − 1 3/5

   a. 1 1/25
   b. 3 3/25
   c. 1 2/5
   d. 2 3/5

29. Simplify 0.25 + 1/3 + 2/3

   a. 1 1/4
   b. 2 1/4
   c. 1 1/3
   d. 2 1/4

30. Brad has agreed to buy everyone a Coke. Each drink costs $1.89, and there are 5 friends. Estimate Brad's cost.

   a. $7
   b. $8
   c. $10
   d. $12

31. Calculate (14 + 2) x 2 + 3

   a. 21
   b. 35
   c. 80
   d. 43

32. 10 x 2 − (7 + 9)

    a. 21

    b. 16

    c. 4

    d. 13

33. Express 5 x 5 x 5 x 5 x 5 x 5 in exponential form.

    a. 5^6

    b. 10^6

    c. 5^{16}

    d. 5^3

34. Express 9 x 9 x 9 in exponential form and standard form.

    a. $9^3 = 719$

    b. $9^3 = 629$

    c. $9^3 = 729$

    d. $10^3 = 729$

35. Solve $3^5 \div 3^8$

    a. 3^3

    b. 3^5

    c. 3^6

    d. 3^4

36. $3^2 \times 3^5$

    a. 3^{17}

    b. 3^5

    c. 4^8

    d. 3^7

37. Brad went for dinner and his bill came to 15.40. He would like to leave a 20% tip. How much is his total bill?

   a. $15.40
   b. $18.48
   c. $17.48
   d. $19.05

38. Sandra makes 15.00 per hour and works a 35 hour week. How much does she make in 1 month? Assume 1 month has 4 weeks.

   a. $2,000
   b. $2,200
   c. $2,100
   d. $1,900

39. Mark borrows $5,000 from the bank to buy a new car. The interest rate is 7%. How much is the total cost of the loan?

   a. $5,000
   b. $5350
   c. $5500
   c. $5250

40. Carli needs to buy carpet for her bedroom, which is 10 feet by 15 feet. How many square feet of carpet should she order?

   a. 100 sq. ft.
   b. 125 sq. ft.
   c. 150 sq. ft.
   c. 200 sq. ft.

Part III - Vocabulary

Choose the word that matches the given definition.

1. An exit or way out is a/an

    a. Door-jamb
    b. Egress
    c. Regress
    d. Furtherance

2. Something private or personal is

    a. Confidential
    b. Hysteric
    c. Simplistic
    d. Promissory

3. A serious criminal offence that is punishable by death or imprisonment above a year, is a

    a. Trespass
    b. Hampers
    c. Felony
    d. Obligatory

4. VERB To encourage or incite to trouble is to

    a. Comment
    b. Foment
    c. Integument
    d. Atonement

5. A dignified and solemn manner that is appropriate for a funeral, is

   a. Funereal
   b. Prediction
   c. Wailing
   d. Vociferous

6. A warm and kind person is.

   a. Seethe
   b. Geniality
   c. Desists
   d. Predicate

7. A polite and well mannered person is

   a. Chivalrous
   b. Hilarious
   c. Genteel
   d. Governance

8. To encourage, stimulate or incite and provoke is to

   a. Push
   b. Force
   c. Threaten
   d. Goad

9. Something shocking, terrible or wicked is

   a. Pleasantries
   b. Heinous
   c. Shrewd
   d. Provencal

10. ADJECTIVE Common, not honorable or noble.

   a. Princely
   b. Ignoble
   c. Shameful
   d. Sham

11. Something irrelevant is

   a. Immaterial
   b. Prohibition
   c. Prediction
   d. Brokerage

12. Something perfect, with no faults or errors is

   a. Impeccable
   b. Formidable
   c. Genteel
   d. Disputation

13. The ruling council of a military government is a/an

   a. Sophist
   b. Counsel
   c. Virago
   d. Junta

14. Someone of influence, rank or distinction, is a/an

   a. Consummate
   b. Sinister
   c. Accolade
   d. Magnate

15. Quick and light in movement is

   a. Quickest
   b. Nimble
   c. Rapacious
   d. Perspicuities

16. A loud unpleasant noise is a/an

   a. Nosy
   b. Racket
   c. Ravage
   d. Noisome

17. Something relating to a wedding or marriage is a

   a. Nefarious
   b. Fluctuate
   c. Nuptial
   d. Flatulence

18. Something Open to display or apparent is

   a. Ostensible
   b. Complacent
   c. Hidden
   d. Harrowing

19. Someone appearing weak or pale is

   a. Pallid
   b. Palliative
   c. Deviant
   d. Expatiate

20. A picture or series of pictures representing a continuous scene is a

   a. Accolade
   b. Obdurate
   c. Panorama
   d. Personification

21. A self contradictory statement is a

   a. Inbred
   b. Paradox
   c. Attribute
   d. Fealty

22. A question or inquiry is a

   a. Cite
   b. Query
   c. Linger
   d. Gibe

23. A deep narrow valley or gorge cause by running water is a

   a. Rumbling
   b. Ravine
   c. Delectable
   d. Distraught

24. To move back or away is to

   a. Implicate
   b. Oscillate
   c. Recede
   d. Meander

25. To To become wrinkled is to

   a. Sheave
   b. Shrivel
   c. Vernal
   d. Meticulous

26. A place where leather is made is a

   a. Shrapnel
   b. Leathery
   c. Tannery
   d. Malleable

27. Complete agreement or harmony is

   a. Ambiguous
   b. Unanimous
   c. Adulate
   d. Incredulous

28. Using humor to exaggerate or ridicule someone is,

   a. Satire
   b. Humor
   c. Recognition
   d. Irony

29. An uncertain or inexact meaning is called

   a. Ambiguity
   b. Nefarious
   c. Rapacious
   d. Shrewd

30. Lacking proper respect and seriousness is

   a. Obdurate
   b. Consummate
   c. Promissory
   d. Irreverent

31. Friendship; peaceful harmony.

   a. Amity
   b. Palliative
   c. Chivalrous
   d. Nebulous

32. Commonplace; tired or petty is

   a. Obdurate
   b. Distraught
   c. Banal
   d. Meticulous

33. A lamentable, dreadful, or fatal event or affair; calamity;

   a. Tragedy
   b. Epic
   c. Sonnet
   d. Tall Tale

34. Distress or embarrassment is

   a. Complacent
   b. Chagrin
   c. Nefarious
   d. Predicate

35. To shake or wave, is to

   a. Occilate
   b. Osculate
   c. Brandish
   d. Avert

36. Fearless, intrepid or bold is

   a. Meticulous
   b. Dauntless
   c. Ambiguous
   d. Shrivel

37. A large, powerful, or violent whirlpool is a

   a. Maelstrom
   b. Tornado
   c. Tsunami
   d. Undertow

38. The actions of a criminal are,

   a. Palliative
   b. Nefarious
   c. Deviant
   d. Obdurate

39. Lacking care or attention to duty is

   a. Remiss
   b. Forgetful
   c. Ostensible
   d. Rumbling

40. Contrary to reason or common sense is

   a. Adventurous
   b. Preposterous
   c. Anonymous
   d. Exceptional

Practice Test 1

Answer Key

Part 1 – Reading Comprehension

1. A
Helen's parents hired Anne to teach Helen to communicate. Choice B is incorrect because the passage states Anne had trouble finding her way around, which means she could walk. Choice C is incorrect because you don't hire a teacher to teach someone to play. Choice D is incorrect because by age 6, if Helen had never eaten, she would have starved to death.

2. B
The correct answer because that fact is stated directly in the passage. The passage explains that Anne taught Helen to hear by allowing her to feel the vibrations in her throat.

3. A
We can infer that Anne is a patient teacher because she did not leave or lose her temper when Helen bit or hit her; she just kept trying to teach Helen. Choice B is incorrect because Anne taught Helen to read and talk. Choice C is incorrect because Anne could hear. She was partially blind, not deaf. Choice D is incorrect because it does not have to do with patience.

4. B
The passage states that it was hard for anyone but Anne to understand Helen when she spoke. Choice A is incorrect because the passage does not mention Helen spoke a foreign language. Choice C is incorrect because there is no mention of how quiet or loud Helen's voice was. Choice D is incorrect because we know from reading the passage that Helen did learn to speak.

5. D
This question tests the reader's summarization skills. The question is asking very generally about the message of the passage, and the title, "Ways Characters Communicate in Theater," is one indication of that. The other choices A, B, and C are all directly from the text, and therefore readers

may be inclined to select one of them, but are too specific to encapsulate the entirety of the passage and its message.

6. B
The paragraph on soliloquies mentions "To be or not to be," and it is from the context of that paragraph that readers may understand that because "To be or not to be" is a soliloquy, Hamlet will be introspective, or thoughtful, while delivering it. It is true that actors deliver soliloquies alone, and may be "solitary" (choice A), but "thoughtful" (choice B) is more true to the overall idea of the paragraph. Readers may choose C because drama and theater can be used interchangeably and the passage mentions that soliloquies are unique to theater (and therefore drama), but this answer is not specific enough to the paragraph in question. Readers may pick up on the theme of life and death and Hamlet's true intentions and select that he is "hopeless" (choice D), but those themes are not discussed either by this paragraph or passage, as a close textual reading and analysis confirms.

7. C
This question tests the reader's grammatical skills. Choice B seems logical, but parenthesis are actually considered to be a stronger break in a sentence than commas are, and along this line of thinking, actually disrupt the sentence more.

Choices A and D make comparisons between theater and film that are not made in the passage, and may or may not be true. This detail does clarify the statement that asides are most unique to theater by adding that it is not completely unique to theater, which may have been why the author didn't chose not to delete it and instead used parentheses to designate the detail's importance (choice C).

8. A
Low blood sugar occurs both in diabetics and healthy adults.

9. B
None of the statements are the author's opinion.

10. A
The author's purpose is the inform.

PRACTICE TEST 1

11. A
The only statement that is not a detail is, "A doctor can diagnosis this medical condition by asking the patient questions and testing."

12. A
This sentence is a recommendation.

13. C
Tips for a good night's sleep is the best alternative title for this article.

14. B
Mental activity is helpful for a good night's sleep is can not be inferred from this article.

15. A
From the passage, one disadvantage of taking naps is they may keep you awake at night.

16. C
To be infamous means to be remembered for an evil or terrible action. Therefore, the word infamy means to remember a bad or terrible thing. Choice A is incorrect because being famous is not the same as being infamous. Choice B is incorrect because the attack on Pearl Harbor was not good. Choice D is incorrect because Pearl Harbor was not forgotten.

17. C
Each other answer set contains the name of at least one country that was not part of the AXIS powers.

18. D
It is stated in the passage. Choice A is not correct because there was no indication that Japan would attack San Diego Choice B is incorrect because the attack on Pearl Harbor was a surprise. Choice C is incorrect because Roosevelt was not planning to attack Japan.

19. C
The passage clearly states that Japan planned a surprise attack. They chose that early time to catch the U.S. military off guard. Choice A is incorrect because the military does

not sleep late. Choice B is incorrect because there is no law against bombing countries. Choice D is incorrect because it makes no sense.

20. C
This question tests the reader's vocabulary skills. The uses of the negatives "but" and "less," especially right next to each other, may confuse readers into answering with choices A or D, which list words that are antonyms to "militant." Readers may also be confused by the comparison of healthy people with what is being described as an overly healthy person-- both people are good, but the reader may look for which one is "worse" in the comparison, and therefore stray toward the antonym words. One key to understanding the meaning of "militant" if the reader is unfamiliar with it is to look at the root of the word; readers can then easily associate it with "military" and gain a sense of what the word signifies: defence (especially considered that the immune system defends the body). Choice C is correct over choice B because "militant" is an adjective, just as the words in choice C are, whereas the words in choice B are nouns.

21. C
This question tests the reader's understanding of function within writing. The other choices are details included surrounding the quoted text, and may therefore confuse the reader. Choice A somewhat contradicts what is said earlier in the paragraph, which is that tests and treatments are improving, and probably doctors are along with them, but the paragraph doesn't actually mention doctors, and the subject of the question is the medicine. Choice B may seem correct to readers who aren't careful to understand that, while the author does mention the large number of people affected, the author is touching on the realities of living with allergies, rather than the likelihood of curing all allergies. Similarly, while the author does mention the "balance" of the body, which is easily associated with "wholesome," the author is not really making an argument and especially is not making an extreme statement that allergy medicines should be outlawed. Again, because the article's tone is on living with allergies, choice C is an appropriate choice that fits with the title and content of the text.

22. B

This question tests the reader's inference skills. The text does not state who is doing the recommending, but the use of the "patients," as well as the general context of the passage, lends itself to the logical partner, "doctors," choice B. The author does mention the recommendation but doesn't present it as her own (i.e. "I recommend that"), so choice A may be eliminated. It may seem plausible that people with allergies (choice D) may recommend medicines or products to other people with allergies, but the text does not necessarily support this interaction taking place. Choice C may be selected because the EpiPen is specifically mentioned, but the use of the phrase "such as" when it is introduced is not limiting enough to assume the recommendation is coming from its creators.

23. D

This question tests the reader's global understanding of the text. Choice D includes the main topics of the three body paragraphs, and isn't too focused on a specific aspect or quote from the text, as the other questions are, giving a skewed summary of what the author intended. The reader may be drawn to choice B because of the title of the passage and the use of words like "better," but the message of the passage is larger and more general than this.

24. B

Reading the document posted to the Human Resources website is optional.

25. B

The document is recommended changes and have not be implemented yet.

26. C

This question tests the reader's summarization skills. The use of the word "actually" in describing what kind of people poets are, as well as other moments like this, may lead readers to selecting choices B or D, but the author is more information than trying to persuade readers. The author gives no indication that she loves poetry (choice B) or that people, students specifically (D), should write poems. Choice A is incorrect because the style and content of this paragraph do not match those of a foreword; forewords usually focus on the history or ideas of a specific poem to introduce it more fully and help it stand out against other poems. The author here focuses on several poems and gives broad statements. Instead, she tells a kind of story about poems, giving three very broad time periods in which to discuss them, thereby giving a brief history of poetry, as choice C states.

27. A
This question tests the reader's summarization skills. Key words in the topic sentences of each of the paragraphs ("oldest," "Renaissance," "modern") should give the reader an idea that the author is moving chronologically. The opening and closing sentence-paragraphs are broad and talk generally. B seems reasonable, but epic poems are mentioned in two paragraphs, eliminating the idea that only new types of poems are used in each paragraph. Choice C is also easily eliminated because the author clearly mentions several different poets, groups of people, and poems. Choice D also seems reasonable, considering that the author does move from older forms of poetry to newer forms, but use of "so (that)" makes this statement false, for the author gives no indication that she is rushing (the paragraphs are about the same size) or that she prefers modern poetry.

28. D
This question tests the reader's attention to detail. The key word is "invented"-- it ties together the Mesopotamians, who invented the written word, and the fact that they, as the inventors, also invented and used poetry. The other selections focus on other details mentioned in the passage, such as that the Renaissance's admiration of the Greeks (choice C) and that Beowulf is in Old English (choice A). Choice B may seem like an attractive answer because it is unlike the others and because the idea of heroes seems rooted in ancient and early civilizations.

29. B
This question tests the reader's vocabulary and contextualization skills. "Telling" is not an unusual word, but it may be used here in a way that is not familiar to readers, as an adjective rather than a verb in gerund form. Choice A may seem like the obvious answer to a reader looking for a verb to match the use they are familiar with. If the reader under-

stands that the word is being used as an adjective and that choice A is a ploy, they may opt to select choice D, "wordy," but it does not make sense in context. Choice C can be easily eliminated, and doesn't have any connection to the paragraph or passage. "Significant" (choice B) makes sense contextually, especially relative to the phrase "give insight" used later in the sentence.

30. C
Wind is the highest source of renewable energy in Scotland. The other choices are either not mentioned at all or not mentioned in the context for how fast they are growing.

Part II – Number Operations

1. A
1/3 X 3/4 = 3/12 = 1/4

2. D
75/1500 = 15/300 = 3/60 = 1/20

3. D
3.14 + 2.73 = 5.87 and 5.87 + 23.7 = 29.57

4. B
She spent 15% so, 100% - 15% = 85%

5. C
To convert a decimal to a fraction, take the places of decimal as your denominator, here, 2, so in 0.27, '7' is in the 100th place, so the fraction is 27/100 and 0.33 becomes 33/100.

Next estimate the answer quickly to eliminate obvious wrong choices. 27/100 is about 1/4 and 33/100 is 1/3. 1/3 is slightly larger than 1/4, and 1/4 + 1/4 is 1/2, so the answer will be slightly larger than 1/2.

Looking at the choices, Choice A can be eliminated since 3/6 = 1/2. Choice D, 2/7 is less than 1/2 and can be eliminated. so the answer is going to be Choice B or Choice C.
Do the calculation, 0.27 + 0.33 = 0.60 and 0.60 = 60/100 =

3/5, Choice C is correct.

6. D
3.13 + 7.87 = 11 and 11 X 5 = 55

7. B
2/4 X 3/4 = 6/16, and reduced to the lowest terms = 3/8

8. D
2/3-2/5 = 10-6 /15 = 4/15

9. C
2/7 + 2/3 = 6+14 /21 (21 is the common denominator) = 20/21

10. B
2/3 x 60 = 40 and 1.5 x 75 = 15, 40 + 15 = 55

11. C
This is an easy question, and shows how you can solve some questions without doing the calculations. The question is, 8 is what percent of 40. Take easy percentages for an approximate answer and see what you get.

10% is easy to calculate because you can drop the zero, or move the decimal point. 10% of 40 = 4, and 8 = 2 X 4, so, 8 must be 2 X 10% = 20%.

Here are the calculations which confirm the quick approximation.
8/40 = X/100 = 8 * 100 / 40X = 800/40 = X = 20

12. D
This is the same type of question which illustrates another method to solve quickly without doing the calculations. The question is, 9 is what percent of 36?

Ask, what is the relationship between 9 and 36? 9 X 4 = 36 so they are related by a factor of 4. If 9 is related to 36 by a factor of 4, then what is related to 100 (to get a percent) by a factor of 4?

To visualize:

9 X 4 = 36
Z X 4 = 100

So the answer is 25. 9 has the same relation to 36 as 25 has to 100.

Here are the calculations which confirm the quick approximation.
9/36 = X/100 = 9 * 100 / 36X = 900/36 = 25

13. C
3/10 * 90 = 3 * 90/10 = 27

14. B
4/100 * 36 = .4 * 36/100 = .144

15. B
$(4)(3)^3 = (4)(27) = 108$

16. D
To solve for x,
5x – 7x + 3 = -1
5x – 7x = -1 -3
-2x = -4
x = -4/ -2
x = 2

17. C
To solve for x, first simplify the equation
5x + 2x + 14 = 14x – 7
7x + 14 = 4x -7
7x – 14x + 14 = -7
7x – 14x = -7 – 14
-7x = -21
x = -21/-7
x = 3

18. A
5z + 5 = 3z +6 + 11
5z -3z + 5 =6 + 11
5z – 3z = 6 + 11 -5
2z = 17 – 5

2z = 12
z = 12/2
z = 6

19. C
5z + 5 = 3z +6 + 11
5z -3z + 5 = 6 + 11
5z – 3z = 6 + 11 -5
2z = 17 – 5
2z = 12
z = 12/2
z = 6

20. D
The price increased by $5 ($25-$20). The percent increase is 5/20 x 100 = 5 x 5=25%

21. C
The price decreased by $5 ($25-$20). The percent increase = 5/25 x 100 = 5 x 4 =20%

22. D
The price of all the single items is same and there are 13 total items. So the total cost will be 13 × 1.3 = $16.9. After 3.5 percent tax this amount will become 16.9 × 1.035 = $17.5.

23. B
$X/2 - 250 = 3X/7$
X = $3500

24. B
Actual cost = X, therefore, 545 = x + 0.15x, 545 = 1x + 0.15x, 545 = 1.15x, x = 545/1.15 = 473.9.

25. C
Initial cost was $220, so the new cost = 220 + (45% of 220). 45% of 220 = 45/100 * X/220 = 99, therefore new price is 220 + 99 = $319

26. D
Let the old salary = X, therefore $150 = x + 0.30x, 150 = 1x + 0.30x, 150 = 1.30x, x = 150/1.30 = 115.4

27. D
700,653 − 70,099 = 630,0554

28. B
0.12 + 2/5 + 3/5, Convert decimal to fraction to get 3/25 + (1 2/5 = 7/5 = 35/25) + (1 3/5 = 8/5 = 40/25), = (3 + 35 + 40)/25, = 78/25 = 3 3/25

29. A
0.25 + 2 1/3 + 2/3, first convert decimal to fraction, 1/4 + 1/3 + 2/3, (3 + 4 + 8)/12, = 15/12 = 5/4 = 1 1/4

30. C
If there are 5 friends and each drink costs $1.89, we can round up to $2 per drink and estimate the total cost at, 5 X $2 = $10.
The actual cost is 5 X $1.89 = $9.45.

31. B
(14 + 2) x 2 + 3 = 35. Order or operations, do brackets first, then multiplication and division, then addition and subtraction.

32. C
10 x 2 − (7 + 9) = 4. This is an order of operations question. Do the brackets first, then multiplication and division, then addition and subtraction.

33. A
5^6

34. C
Exponential form is 9^3 and standard from is 729

35. A
To divide exponents with the same base, subtract the exponents. $3^{8-5} = 3^3$

36. D
When multiplying exponents with the same base, add the exponents. $3^2 \times 3^5 = 3^{2+5} = 3^7$

37. B
The meal was 15.40 and the tip 20%, so the total will be $15.40 + (15.40 * 20%).

Let the amount of the tip be X. So, x/15.40 = 20/100
100x = 15.40 * 20
100x = 308
x = 308/100 = 3.08 (amount of the tip)
The total will be 15.40 + 3.08 = $18.48

38. C
First calculate how much she will make in a week and then multiply that number by 4 to reach the total for one month.

$15 X 35 = 525 (earnings for 1 week)
525 * 4 = $2,100

39. B
The total cost will be the original amount ($5,000) plus the interest, which will be 5000 * 7%.

To calculate the interest, x/5000 * 7/100

100x = 5000 * 7
100x = 35,000
x = 35,000/100 (Cancel zeros)
x = 350 (amount of interest)

So the total cost of the loan will be $5,000 + $350 = $5350.

40. C
The room is 10 X 15, so to find the square footage, multiply. 10 * 15 = 150 square feet.

Part III - Vocabulary

1. B
Egress NOUN an exit or way out.

2. A
Confidential ADJECTIVE kept secret within a certain circle of persons; not intended to be known publicly.

3. C
Felony NOUN serious criminal offence that is punishable by death or imprisonment above a year.

4. B
Foment VERB to encourage or incite troublesome acts.

5. A
Funereal ADJECTIVE dignified, solemn that is appropriate for a funeral.

6. B
Geniality NOUN warmth and kindness of disposition.

7. C
Genteel ADJECTIVE polite and well mannered.

8. D
Goad VERB to encourage, stimulate or incite and provoke.

9. B
Heinous ADJECTIVE shocking, terrible or wicked.

10. B
Ignoble ADJECTIVE common, not honorable or noble.

11. A
Immaterial ADJECTIVE irrelevant not having substance or matter.

12. A
Impeccable ADJECTIVE perfect, no faults or errors.

13. D
Junta NOUN ruling council of a military government.

14. D
Magnate NOUN a person of influence, rank or distinction.

15. B
Nimble ADJECTIVE quick and light in movement.

16. B
Racket NOUN a loud noise.

17. C
Nuptial NOUN of or pertaining to wedding and marriage.

18. A
Ostensible ADJECTIVE meant for open display; apparent.

19. A
Pallid ADJECTIVE appearing weak, pale, or wan.

20. C
Panorama NOUN a picture or series of pictures representing a continuous scene.

21. B
Paradox NOUN a self contradictory statement that can only be true if false and vice versa.

22. B
Query NOUN question or inquiry.

23. B
Ravine NOUN a deep narrow valley or gorge in the earth's surface worn by running water.

24. C
Recede VERB move back or move away.

25. B
Shrivel VERB to become wrinkled.

26. C
Tannery NOUN a place where people tan hides to make leather.

27. B
Unanimous ADJECTIVE complete agreement or harmony.

28. A
Satire NOUN using humor to exaggerate or ridicule someone or something.

29. A
Ambiguity NOUN an uncertain or inexact meaning.

30. D
Irreverent (adjective) Lacking proper respect and seriousness.

31. A
Amity NOUN friendship; peaceful harmony.

32. C
Banal ADJECTIVE Commonplace; tired or petty.

33. A
Tragedy NOUN a lamentable, dreadful, or fatal event or affair; calamity.

34. B
Chagrin Noun distress or embarrassment

35. C
Brandish VERB to shake or wave, as a weapon; flourish

36. B
Dauntless ADJECTIVE fearless; intrepid; bold.

37. A
Maelstrom NOUN A large, powerful, or violent whirlpool.

38. B
Nefarious ADJECTIVE (typically of an action or activity) wicked or criminal.

39. A
Remiss ADJECTIVE Lacking care or attention to duty.

40. B
Preposterous ADJECTIVE Contrary to reason or common sense.

Rounding the Final Corner Practice Test 2

You've made it to the second practice test! By now, you've likely reviewed your notes from the first round and spent some time smoothing out those rough patches in math or vocabulary. This second test is your chance to see how far you've come.

Just a reminder: these questions aren't carbon copies of the ones you'll see on test day. The folks who design the CAAT like to keep us on our toes by switching things up, adjusting time limits, or rearranging sections. But don't let that get under your skin. We've built these questions to reflect the same level of difficulty and the same core concepts as the real exam. If you can stay cool and work through these, you're in great shape for the real thing.

Treat This Like the "Dress Rehearsal"
Now is the time to really mimic the exam environment. No "checking the formula sheet" or taking a quick break to answer a text.

The "Exam Zone": Find that quiet spot—the library, a back room, or the kitchen table after the house has gone quiet. Clear away everything except your pencil, your eraser, and your bubble sheet.

Read Twice, Answer Once: It's easy to rush when you're familiar with the material. Slow down. Make sure you understand exactly what the question is asking before you commit to an answer.

Trust Your Training: You've been working through the tutorials and building your word lists. Trust those instincts. If a math problem looks tough, take a breath and break it down into the smaller parts we practiced.

The "Post-Game" Review: Once the timer hits zero, take a break before you grade yourself. When you do look at the Answer Key, pay close attention to the explanations. Even if you got a question right, seeing why it's right helps lock that knowledge in.

One Step at a Time
I can't stress this enough: don't rush into the next test. If you find yourself wanting to do Test #2 and Test #3 back-to-back, take a walk instead. Your brain needs time to "digest" what it learned from this session. Give it another 48 to 72 hours before you tackle the final sets of questions.

You're doing the work, and it's going to pay off. Focus on the page in front of you, stay steady, and let's see what you can do.

Reading Comprehension Answer Sheet

	A	B	C	D	E		A	B	C	D	E
1	○	○	○	○	○	21	○	○	○	○	○
2	○	○	○	○	○	22	○	○	○	○	○
3	○	○	○	○	○	23	○	○	○	○	○
4	○	○	○	○	○	24	○	○	○	○	○
5	○	○	○	○	○	25	○	○	○	○	○
6	○	○	○	○	○	26	○	○	○	○	○
7	○	○	○	○	○	27	○	○	○	○	○
8	○	○	○	○	○	28	○	○	○	○	○
9	○	○	○	○	○	29	○	○	○	○	○
10	○	○	○	○	○	30	○	○	○	○	○
11	○	○	○	○	○	31	○	○	○	○	○
12	○	○	○	○	○	32	○	○	○	○	○
13	○	○	○	○	○	33	○	○	○	○	○
14	○	○	○	○	○	34	○	○	○	○	○
15	○	○	○	○	○	35	○	○	○	○	○
16	○	○	○	○	○	36	○	○	○	○	○
17	○	○	○	○	○	37	○	○	○	○	○
18	○	○	○	○	○	38	○	○	○	○	○
19	○	○	○	○	○	39	○	○	○	○	○
20	○	○	○	○	○	40	○	○	○	○	○

Number Operations Answer Sheet

	A	B	C	D	E		A	B	C	D	E
1	○	○	○	○	○	21	○	○	○	○	○
2	○	○	○	○	○	22	○	○	○	○	○
3	○	○	○	○	○	23	○	○	○	○	○
4	○	○	○	○	○	24	○	○	○	○	○
5	○	○	○	○	○	25	○	○	○	○	○
6	○	○	○	○	○	26	○	○	○	○	○
7	○	○	○	○	○	27	○	○	○	○	○
8	○	○	○	○	○	28	○	○	○	○	○
9	○	○	○	○	○	29	○	○	○	○	○
10	○	○	○	○	○	30	○	○	○	○	○
11	○	○	○	○	○						
12	○	○	○	○	○						
13	○	○	○	○	○						
14	○	○	○	○	○						
15	○	○	○	○	○						
16	○	○	○	○	○						
17	○	○	○	○	○						
18	○	○	○	○	○						
19	○	○	○	○	○						
20	○	○	○	○	○						

Vocabulary Answer Sheet

	A	B	C	D	E		A	B	C	D	E
1	○	○	○	○	○	21	○	○	○	○	○
2	○	○	○	○	○	22	○	○	○	○	○
3	○	○	○	○	○	23	○	○	○	○	○
4	○	○	○	○	○	24	○	○	○	○	○
5	○	○	○	○	○	25	○	○	○	○	○
6	○	○	○	○	○	26	○	○	○	○	○
7	○	○	○	○	○	27	○	○	○	○	○
8	○	○	○	○	○	28	○	○	○	○	○
9	○	○	○	○	○	29	○	○	○	○	○
10	○	○	○	○	○	30	○	○	○	○	○
11	○	○	○	○	○	31	○	○	○	○	○
12	○	○	○	○	○	32	○	○	○	○	○
13	○	○	○	○	○	33	○	○	○	○	○
14	○	○	○	○	○	34	○	○	○	○	○
15	○	○	○	○	○	35	○	○	○	○	○
16	○	○	○	○	○	36	○	○	○	○	○
17	○	○	○	○	○	37	○	○	○	○	○
18	○	○	○	○	○	38	○	○	○	○	○
19	○	○	○	○	○	39	○	○	○	○	○
20	○	○	○	○	○	40	○	○	○	○	○

Part I - Reading Comprehension

Questions 1 - 4 refer to the following passage.

Passage 1 - The Crusades

In 1095 Pope Urban II proclaimed the First Crusade with the intent and stated goal to restore Christian access to holy places in and around Jerusalem. Over the next 200 years there were 6 major crusades and numerous minor crusades in the fight for control of the "Holy Land." Historians are divided on the real purpose of the Crusades, some believing that it was part of a purely defensive war against Islamic conquest; some see them as part of a long-running conflict at the frontiers of Europe; and others see them as confident, aggressive, papal-led expansion attempts by Western Christendom. The impact of the crusades was profound, and judgment of the Crusaders ranges from laudatory to highly critical. However, all agree that the Crusades and wars waged during those crusades were brutal and often bloody. Several hundred thousand Roman Catholic Christians joined the Crusades, they were Christians from all over Europe.

Europe at the time was under the Feudal System, so, while the Crusaders made vows to the Church, they also were beholden to their Feudal Lords. This led to the Crusaders not only fighting the Saracen, the commonly used word for Muslim at the time, but also each other for power and economic gain in the Holy Land. This infighting between the Crusaders is why many historians hold the view that the Crusades were simply a front for Europe to invade the Holy Land for economic gain in the name of the Church. Another factor contributing to this theory is that while the army of crusaders marched towards Jerusalem they pillaged the land as they went. The church and feudal Lords vowing to return the land to its original beauty, and inhabitants, this rarely happened though, as the Lords often kept the land for themselves. A full 800 years after the Crusades, Pope John Paul II expressed his sorrow for the massacre of innocent people and the lasting damage that the Medieval church caused.

1. What is the tone of this article?

    a. Subjective

    b. Objective

    c. Persuasive

    d. None of the Above

2. What can all historians agree on concerning the Crusades?

    a. It achieved great things

    b. It stabilized the Holy Land

    c. It was bloody and brutal

    d. It helped defend Europe from the Byzantine Empire

3. What impact did the feudal system have on the Crusades?

    a. It unified the Crusaders

    b. It helped gather volunteers

    c. It had no effect on the Crusades

    d. It led to infighting, causing more damage than good

4. What does Saracen mean?

    a. Muslim

    b. Christian

    c. Knight

    d. Holy Land

Questions 5 - 8 refer to the following passage.

ABC Electric Warranty

ABC Electric Company warrants that its products are free from defects in material and workmanship. Subject to the conditions and limitations set forth below, ABC Electric will, at its option, either repair or replace any part of its products that prove defective due to improper workmanship or materials.

This limited warranty does not cover any damage to the product from improper installation, accident, abuse, misuse, natural disaster, insufficient or excessive electrical supply, abnormal mechanical or environmental conditions, or any unauthorized disassembly, repair, or modification.

This limited warranty also does not apply to any product on which the original identification information has been altered, or removed, has not been handled or packaged correctly, or has been sold as second-hand.

This limited warranty covers only repair, replacement, refund or credit for defective ABC Electric products, as provided above.

5. I tried to repair my ABC Electric blender, but could not, so can I get it repaired under this warranty?

    a. Yes, the warranty still covers the blender

    b. No, the warranty does not cover the blender

    c. Uncertain. ABC Electric may or may not cover repairs under this warranty

6. My ABC Electric fan is not working. Will ABC Electric provide a new one or repair this one?

    a. ABC Electric will repair my fan

    b. ABC Electric will replace my fan

    c. ABC Electric could either replace or repair my fan can request either a replacement or a repair.

7. My stove was damaged in a flood. Does this warranty cover my stove?

    a. Yes, it is covered.

    b. No, it is not covered.

    c. It may or may not be covered.

    d. ABC Electric will decide if it is covered

8. Which of the following is an example of improper workmanship?

    a. Missing parts

    b. Defective parts

    c. Scratches on the front

    d. None of the above

Questions 9 – 12 refer to the following passage.

Passage 2 - Women and Advertising

Only in the last few generations have media messages been so widespread and so readily seen, heard, and read by so many people. Advertising is an important part of both selling and buying anything from soap to cereal to jeans. For whatever reason, more consumers are women than are men. Media message are subtle but powerful, and more attention has been paid lately to how these message affect women. Of all the products that women buy, makeup, clothes, and other stylistic or cosmetic products are among the most popular. This means that companies focus their advertising on women, promising them that their product will make her feel, look, or smell better than the next company's product will. This competition has resulted in advertising that is more and more ideal and less and less possible for everyday women. However, because women do look to these ideals and the products they represent as how they can potentially become, many women have developed unhealthy attitudes about themselves when they have failed to become those ideals.

In recent years, more companies have tried to change advertisements to be healthier for women. This includes featuring models of more sizes and addressing a huge outcry against unfair tools such as airbrushing and photo editing. There is debate about what the right balance between real and ideal is, because fashion is also considered art and some changes are made to elevate fashionable products purposefully and signify that they are creative, innovative, and the work of individual people. Artists want their freedom protected as much as women do, and advertising agencies are often caught in the middle.

Some claim that the companies who make these changes are not doing enough. Many people worry that there are still not enough models of different sizes and different ethnicities. Some people claim that companies use this healthier type of advertisement not for the good of women, but because they would like to sell products to the women who are looking for these kinds of messages. This is also a hard balance to find: companies need to make money, and women need to feel respected.
While the focus of this change has been on women, advertising can also affect men, and this change will hopefully be a lesson on media for all consumers.

9. The second paragraph states that advertising focuses on women

    a. to shape what the ideal should be

    b. because women buy makeup

    c. because women are easily persuaded

    d. because of the types of products that women buy

10. According to the passage, fashion artists and female consumers are at odds because

   a. there is a debate going on and disagreement drives people apart

   b. both of them are trying to protect their freedom to do something

   c. artists want to elevate their products above the reach of women

   d. women are creative, innovative, individual people

11. The author uses the phrase "for whatever reason" in this passage to

   a. keep the focus of the paragraph on media messages and not on the differences between men and women

   b. show that the reason for this is unimportant

   c. argue that it is stupid that more women are consumers than men

   d. show that he or she is tired of talking about why media messages are important

12. This passage suggests that

   a. advertising companies are still working on making their messages better

   b. all advertising companies seek to be more approachable for women

   c. women are only buying from companies that respect them

   d. artists could stop producing fashionable products if they feel bullied

Questions 13 - 16 refer to the following passage.

FDR, the Treaty of Versailles, and the Fourteen Points

At the conclusion of World War I, those who had won the war and those who were forced to admit defeat welcomed the end of the war and expected that a peace treaty would be signed. The American president, Franklin D. Roosevelt, played an important part in proposing what the agreements should be and did so through his Fourteen Points.

World War I had begun in 1914 when an Austrian archduke was assassinated, leading to a domino effect that pulled the world's most powerful countries into war on a large scale. The war catalysed the creation and use of deadly weapons that had not previously existed, resulting in a great loss of soldiers on both sides of the fighting. More than 9 million soldiers were killed.

The United States agreed to enter the war right before it ended, and many believed that its decision to become finally involved brought on the end of the war. FDR made it very clear that the U.S. was entering the war for moral reasons and had an agenda focused on world peace. The Fourteen Points were individual goals and ideas (focused on peace, free trade, open communication, and self-reliance) that FDR wanted the power nations to strive for now that the war had ended. He was optimistic and had many ideas about what could be accomplished through, and during the post-war peace. However, FDR's fourteen points were poorly received when he presented them to the leaders of other world powers, many of whom wanted only to help their own countries and to punish the Germans for fueling the war, and they fell by the wayside. World War II was imminent, for Germany lost everything.

Some historians believe that the other leaders who participated in the Treaty of Versailles weren't receptive to the Fourteen Points because World War I was fought almost entirely on European soil, and the United States lost much less than did the other powers. FDR was in a unique position to determine the fate of the war, but doing it on his own terms did not help accomplish his goals. This is only one historical example of how the United State has tried to use its power as an important country, but found itself limited because of geological or ideological factors.

13. The main idea of this passage is that

    a. World War I was unfair because no fighting took place in America

    b. World War II happened because of the Treaty of Versailles

    c. the power the United States has to help other countries also prevents it from helping other countries

    d. Franklin D. Roosevelt was one of the United States' smartest presidents

14. According to the second paragraph, World War I started because

    a. an archduke was assassinated

    b. weapons that were more deadly had been developed

    c. a domino effect of allies agreeing to help one another

    d. the world's most powerful countries were large

15. The author includes the detail that 9 million soldiers were killed

    a. to demonstrate why European leaders were hesitant to accept peace

    b. to show the reader the dangers of deadly weapons

    c. to make the reader think about which countries lost the most soldiers

    d. to demonstrate why World War II was imminent

16. According to this passage, catalysed means

   a. analyzed
   b. sped up
   c. invented
   d. funded

Questions 17 - 20 refer to the following passage.

Chocolate Chip Cookies

3/4 cup sugar
3/4 cup packed brown sugar
1 cup butter, softened
2 large eggs, beaten
1 teaspoon vanilla extract
2 1/4 cups all-purpose flour
1 teaspoon baking soda
3/4 teaspoon salt
2 cups semisweet chocolate chips
If desired, 1 cup chopped pecans, or chopped walnuts.
Preheat oven to 375 degrees.

Mix sugar, brown sugar, butter, vanilla and eggs in a large bowl. Stir in flour, baking soda, and salt. The dough will be very stiff.

Stir in chocolate chips by hand with a sturdy wooden spoon. Add the pecans, or other nuts, if desired. Stir until the chocolate chips and nuts are evenly dispersed.

Drop dough by rounded tablespoonfuls 2 inches apart onto a cookie sheet.

Bake 8 to 10 minutes, or, until light brown. Cookies may look underdone, but they will finish cooking after you take them out of the oven.

17. What is the correct order for adding these ingredients?

    a. Brown sugar, baking soda, chocolate chips
    b. Baking soda, brown sugar, chocolate chips
    c. Chocolate chips, baking soda, brown sugar
    d. Baking soda, chocolate chips, brown sugar

18. What does sturdy mean?

    a. Long
    b. Strong
    c. Short
    d. Wide

19. What does disperse mean?

    a. Scatter
    b. To form a ball
    c. To stir
    d. To beat

20. When can you stop stirring the nuts?

    a. When the cookies are cooked.
    b. When the nuts are evenly distributed.
    c. When the nuts are added.
    d. After the chocolate chips are added.

Questions 21 - 23 refer to the following passage.

Lowest Price Guarantee

Get it for less. Guaranteed!

ABC Electric will beat any advertised price by 10% of the difference.

> 1) If you find a lower advertised price, we will beat it by 10% of the difference.
>
> 2) If you find a lower advertised price within 30 days* of your purchase we will beat it by 10% of the difference.
>
> 3) If our own price is reduced within 30 days* of your purchase, bring in your receipt and we will refund the difference.

*14 days for computers, monitors, printers, laptops, tablets, cellular & wireless devices, home security products, projectors, camcorders, digital cameras, radar detectors, portable DVD players, DJ and pro-audio equipment, and air conditioners.

21. I bought a radar detector 15 days ago and saw an ad for the same model only cheaper. Can I get 10% of the difference refunded?

> a. Yes. Since it is less than 30 days, you can get 10% of the difference refunded.
>
> b. No. Since it is more than 14 days, you cannot get 10% of the difference re-funded.
>
> c. It depends on the cashier.
>
> d. Yes. You can get the difference refunded.

22. I bought a flat-screen TV for $500 10 days ago and found an advertisement for the same TV, at another store, on sale for $400. How much will ABC refund under this guarantee?

    a. $100
    b. $110
    c. $10
    d. $400

23. What is the purpose of this passage?

    a. To inform
    b. To educate
    c. To persuade
    d. To entertain

Questions 24 - 27 refer to the following passage.

Passage 6 - What Is Mardi Gras?

Mardi Gras is fast becoming one of the South's most famous and most celebrated holidays. The word Mardi Gras comes from the French and the literal translation is "Fat Tuesday." The holiday has also been called Shrove Tuesday, due to its associations with Lent. The purpose of Mardi Gras is to celebrate and enjoy before the Lenten season of fasting and repentance begins.

What originated by the French Explorers in New Orleans, Louisiana in the 17th century is now celebrated all over the world. Panama, Italy, Belgium and Brazil all host large scale Mardi Gras celebrations, and many smaller cities and towns celebrate this fun loving Tuesday as well. Usually held in February or early March, Mardi Gras is a day of extravagance, a day for people to eat, drink and be merry, to wear costumes, masks and to dance to jazz music.
The French explorers on the Mississippi River would be in shock today if they saw the opulence of the parades and

floats that grace the New Orleans streets during Mardi Gras these days. Parades in New Orleans are divided by organizations. These are more commonly known as Krewes.

Being a member of a Krewe is quite a task because Krewes are responsible for overseeing the parades. Each Krewe's parade is ruled by a Mardi Gras "King and Queen." The role of the King and Queen is to "bestow" gifts on their adoring fans as the floats ride along the street. They throw doubloons, which is fake money and usually colored green, purple and gold, which are the colors of Mardi Gras. Beads in those color shades are also thrown and cups are thrown as well. Beads are by far the most popular souvenir of any Mardi Gras parade, with each spectator attempting to gather as many as possible.

24. The purpose of Mardi Gras is to

    a. Repent for a month.

    b. Celebrate in extravagant ways.

    c. Be a member of a Krewe.

    d. Explore the Mississippi.

25. From reading the passage we can infer that "Kings and Queens,"

    a. Have to be members of a Krewe.

    b. Have to be French.

    c. Have to know how to speak French.

    d. Have to give away their own money.

26. Which group of people began to hold Mardi Gras celebrations?

    a. Settlers from Italy

    b. Members of Krewes

    c. French explorers

    d. Belgium explorers

27. In the context of the passage, what does spectator mean?

    a. Someone who participates actively

    b. Someone who watches the parade's action

    c. Someone on the parade floats

    d. Someone who does not celebrate Mardi Gras

Questions 28 - 30 refer to the following passage.

Passage 1 - Caterpillars

Butterflies and moths have a three stage life cycle. Caterpillars are the first or laval stage. Caterpillars can be either herbivores, feeding mostly on plants, or carnivores, feeding on other insects. Caterpillars eat continuously. Once they are too big for their body, they shed or molt their skin.

Some caterpillars have symbiotic relationships with other insects. A symbiotic relationship is where different species work together in a way that is either harmful or helpful. Symbiotic relationships are critical to many species and ecosystems.

Some caterpillars and ants have a symbiotic or mutual relationship where both benefit. Ants give some protection, and caterpillars provide the ants with honeydew nectar.

Ants and caterpillars communicate by vibrations through the soil as well as grunting and squeaking. Humans are not able to hear these communications.

28. What do most larvae spend their time doing?

    a. Eating

    b. Sleeping

    c. Communicating with ants.

    d. None of the above

29. Are all caterpillars herbivores?

    a. Yes

    b. No, some eat insects

30. What benefit do larvae get from association with ants?

    a. They do not receive any benefit.

    b. Ants give them protection.

    c. Ants give them food.

    d. Ants give them honeydew secretions.

Section II – Number Operations

1. 8327 – 1278 =

    a. 7149

    b. 7209

    c. 6059

    d. 7049

2. 294 X 21 =

    a. 6017

    b. 6174

    c. 6728

    d. 5679

3. 1278 + 4920 =

    a. 6298
    b. 6108
    c. 6198
    d. 6098

4. 285 * 12 =

    a. 3420
    b. 3402
    c. 3024
    d. 2322

5. 4120 − 3216 =

    a. 903
    b. 804
    c. 904
    d. 1904

6. 2417 + 1004 =

    a. 3401
    b. 4321
    c. 3402
    d. 3421

7. 1440 ÷ 12 =

    a. 122
    b. 120
    c. 110
    d. 132

8. 2713 – 1308 =

    a. 1450
    b. 1445
    c. 1405
    d. 1455

9. Calculate (14 + 2) x 2 + 3

    a. 21
    b. 35
    c. 80
    d. 43

10. The sale price of a car is $12,590, which is 20% off the original price. What is the original price?

    a. $14,310.40
    b. $14,990.90
    c. $15,108.00
    d. $15,737.50

11. Express 25% as a fraction.

    a. 1/4
    b. 7/40
    c. 6/25
    d. 8/28

12. 143 * 4 =

    a. 572
    b. 702
    c. 467
    d. 672

13. Express 125% as a decimal.

    a. .125
    b. 12.5
    c. 1.25
    d. 125

14. Multiply 10^4 by 10^2

    a. 10^8
    b. 10^2
    c. 10^6
    d. 10^{-2}

15. Solve for x: 30 is 40% of x

    a. 60
    b. 90
    c. 85
    d. 75

16. 12½% of x is equal to 50. Solve for x.

    a. 300
    b. 400
    c. 450
    d. 350

17. Express 24/56 as a reduced common fraction.

    a. 4/9
    b. 4/11
    c. 3/7
    d. 3/8

.18. Express 87% as a decimal.

   a. .087
   b. 8.7
   c. .87
   d. 87

19. 60 is 75% of x. Solve for x.

   a. 80
   b. 90
   c. 75
   d. 70

20. 10 x 2 – (7 + 9)

   a. 21
   b. 16
   c. 4
   d. 13

21. 60% of x is 12. Solve for x.

   a. 18
   b. 15
   c. 25
   d. 20

22. Express 71/1000 as a decimal.

   a. .71
   b. .0071
   c. .071
   d. 7.1

23. 3^3 =

    a. $\sqrt{81}$
    b. 81/3
    c. 81
    d. 9

24. 4.7 + .9 + .01 =

    a. 5.5
    b. 6.51
    c. 5.61
    d. 5.7

25. .33 × .59 =

    a. .1947
    b. 1.947
    c. .0197
    d. .1817

26. Calculate 11 + 19 x 2 using the order of operations

    a. 60
    b. 50
    c. 49
    d. 54

27. .84 ÷ .7 =

    a. .12
    b. 12
    c. .012
    d. 1.2

28. What number is in the ten thousandths place in 1.7389?

    a. 1
    b. 8
    c. 9
    d. 3

29. .87 - .48 =

    a. .39
    b. .49
    c. .41
    d. .37

30. Convert 60 feet to inches.

    a. 700 inches
    b. 600 inches
    c. 720 inches
    d. 1,800 inches

31. Which of the following numbers is the largest?

    a. 1
    b. $\sqrt{2}$
    c. 3/2
    d. 4/3

32. Subtract 456,890 from 465,890.

    a. 9,000
    b. 7000
    c. 8970
    d. 8500

33. Susan wants to buy a leather jacket that costs $545.00 and is on sale for 10% off. What is the approximate cost?

    a. $525
    b. $450
    c. $475
    d. $500

34. Solve $\sqrt{121}$

    a. 11
    b. 12
    c. 21
    d. None of the above

35. What is the square root of $\sqrt{36}$

    a. 16
    b. 18
    c. 6
    d. 13

36. Calculate 7 + 2 x (6 + 3) ÷ 3 - 7 using order of operations

    a. 6
    b. 5
    c. 7
    d. 4

37. 1628 / 4 =

    a. 307
    b. 667
    c. 447
    d. 407

38. 46 * 15 =

    a. 590
    b. 690
    c. 490
    d. 790

39. 5575 + 8791

    a. 14,756
    b. 14,566
    c. 14,466
    d. 14,366

40. 6149 / 143 =

    a. 43
    b. 47
    c. 37
    d. 54

Part III - Vocabulary

Choose the best word for the given definition.

1. Use of too many words is

    a. Verbiage
    b. Outspoken
    c. Inveigh
    d. Precarious

2. An aide or assistant is sometimes called a/an

    a. Attache
    b. Influx
    c. Mien

d. Knoll

3. To cause or inflict harm or injury is to

   a. Wreck
   b. Mandible
   c. Tremulous
   d. Juxtapose

4. Someone who is foolish, and without understanding is

   a. Coinage
   b. Witless
   c. Distinctive
   d. Nullify

5. A strong fear of strangers is

   a. Xenophobia
   b. Agoraphobia
   c. Frightful
   d. Genteel

6. The highest point, highest state, or peak, is the

   a. Towering
   b. Flickers
   c. Zenith
   d. Grouse

7. A light wind or gentle breeze is called a

   a. Sea-breeze
   b. Scuttle
   c. Zephyr
   d. Freight

Practice Test 2

8. A self-evident or clear obvious truth is a

   a. Truism
   b. Catharsis
   c. Libertine
   d. Tractable

9. Something beyond what is obvious or evident, is

   a. Ulterior
   b. Sybarite
   c. Torsion
   d. Trenchant

10. Something tasteless or bland is

   a. Obstinate
   b. Morose
   c. Inculpate
   d. Vapid

11. A homeless child or stray is a

   a. Elegy
   b. Waif
   c. Martyr
   d. Palaver

12. A complaint or criticism is a

   a. Obsequies
   b. Whine
   c. Opprobrious
   d. Panacea

13. A subordinate of lesser rank or authority, is a/an

   a. Palliate
   b. Plebeian
   c. Underling
   d. Expiate

14. A young animal that is between 1 and 2 years is a/an

   a. Yearling
   b. Rogue
   c. Gnostic
   d. Billet

15. Lush green vegetation is

   a. Coquette
   b. Verdure
   c. Ennui
   d. Lugubrious

16. A person who is very passionate and fanatic about his specific objectives or beliefs is a/an

   a. Plebeian
   b. Zealot
   c. Progenitor
   d. Iconoclast

17. Dizziness is

   a. Indolence
   b. Percipient
   c. Vertigo
   d. Tenacious

18. Something that is obvious or easy to notice is

    a. Important
    b. Conspicuous
    c. Beautiful
    d. Convincing

19. Someone having a disposition to do good is

    a. Happiness
    b. Courage
    c. Kindness
    d. Benevolence

20. Someone that is full of energy, exuberant and noisy is

    a. Boisterous
    b. Soft
    c. Gentle
    d. Warm

21. To fondle is to

    a. Hold
    b. Caress
    c. Facilitate
    d. Neuter

22. Something that is outstanding in importance is

    a. Momentous
    b. Spurious
    c. Extraordinary
    d. Secede

23. An opponent or enemy is a/an

   a. Antagonist
   b. Protagonist
   c. Sophist
   d. Pugilist

24. An object kept as a reminder of a place or event is a

   a. Monument
   b. Memento
   c. Recurrence
   d. Catharsis

25. Producing harm in a stealthy, often gradual, manner is

   a. Adulterate
   b. Acquiesce
   c. Insidious
   d. Deceitful

26. A route for a journey is a

   a. Schedule
   b. Guidebook
   c. Itinerary
   d. Diary

27. Dignified is

   a. Rich
   b. Noble
   c. Gallant
   d. Illustrious

28. A change or alteration is a

   a. Mutation
   b. Veracity
   c. Oration
   d. Facet

29. To express displeasure or indignation is to

   a. Sanction
   b. Resent
   c. Venerate
   d. Cull

30. Fat, plump and overweight is

   a. Chubby
   b. Corrigible
   c. Heathenish
   d. Peccant

31. Fearful or timid is

   a. Skittish
   b. Pervious
   c. Prefatory
   d. Reparable

32. Harsh or rough sounding is

   a. Rambunctious
   b. Unctuous
   c. Exorbitant
   d. Cardinal

33. Living both on land and in water is

   a. Amicable
   b. Fervid
   c. Amphibious
   d. Frigid

34. A slight degree of difference in anything perceptible to the sense of the mind.

   a. Mien
   b. Nuance
   c. Obsequies
   d. Happenstance

35. The feeling that a person or thing is beneath consideration, worthless, or deserving of scorn.

   a. contempt
   b. scorn
   c. impatience
   d. Boisterous

36. Belief or opinion contrary to orthodox religious beliefs

   a. Heresy
   b. Expiate
   c. Acquiesce
   d. Progenitor

37. Abstinence from alcoholic drink.

   a. Nepotism
   b. Hedonism
   c. Catharsis
   d. Temperance

38. Exaggerated claims or statements not intended to be taken literally.

    a. Irony
    b. Hyperbole
    c. Irascible
    d. Vertigo

39. An idea or meaning suggested by or associated with a word or thing is

    a. Annotation

    b. Connotation

    c. Exhibition

    d. Expostulation

40. Second to last is

    a. Ultimate

    b. Penultimate

    c. Pinnacle

    d. Prefatory

Answer Key

1. A
Choice B is incorrect; the author did not express their opinion on the subject matter. Choice C is incorrect, the author was not trying to prove a point, nor is the author trying to persuade.

2. C
Choice C is correct; historians believe it was brutal and bloody. Choice A is incorrect; there is no consensus that the Crusades achieved great things. Choice B is incorrect; it did not stabilize the Holy Lands. Choice D is incorrect, some historians do believe this was the purpose but not all historians.

3. D
The feudal system led to infighting. Choice A is incorrect, it had the opposite effect. Choice B is incorrect, though this is a good answer, it is not the best answer. The Church asked for volunteers not the Feudal Lords. Choice C is incorrect, it did have an effect on the Crusades.

4. A
Saracen was a generic term for Muslims widely used in Europe during the later medieval era.

5. B
This warranty does not cover a product that you have tried to fix yourself. From paragraph two, "This limited warranty does not cover ... any unauthorized disassembly, repair, or modification. "

6. C
ABC Electric could either replace or repair the fan, provided the other conditions are met. ABC Electric has the option to repair or replace.

7. B
The warranty does not cover a stove damaged in a flood. From the passage, "This limited warranty does not cover any damage to the product from improper installation, accident, abuse, misuse, natural disaster, insufficient or excessive electrical supply, abnormal mechanical or environmental conditions."

A flood is an "abnormal environmental condition," and a natural disaster, so it is not covered.

8. A
A missing part is an example of defective workmanship. This is an error made in the manufacturing process. A defective part is not considered workmanship.

9. D
This question tests the reader's summarization skills. The other choices A, B, and C focus on portions of the second paragraph that are too narrow and do not relate to the specific portion of text in question. The complexity of the sentence may mislead students into selecting one of these answers, but rearranging or restating the sentence will lead the reader to the correct answer. In addition, choice A makes an assumption that may or may not be true about the intentions of the company, choice B focuses on one product rather than the idea of the products, and choice C makes an assumption about women that may or may not be true and is not supported by the text.

10. B
This question tests reader's attention to detail. If a reader selects A, he or she may have picked up on the use of the word "debate" and assumed, very logically, that the two are at odds because they are fighting; however, this is simply not supported in the text. Choice C also uses very specific quotes from the text, but it rearranges and gives them false meaning. The artists want to elevate their creations above the creations of other artists, thereby showing that they are "creative" and "innovative." Similarly, choice D takes phrases straight from the text and rearranges and confuses them. The artists are described as wanting to be "creative, innovative, individual people," not the women.

11. A
This question tests reader's vocabulary and summarization skills. This phrase, used by the author, may seem flippant and dismissive if readers focus on the word "whatever" and misinterpret it as a popular, colloquial term. In this way, choices B and C may mislead the reader to selecting one of them by including the terms "unimportant" and "stupid,"

respectively. Choice D is a similar misreading, but doesn't make sense when the phrase is at the beginning of the passage and the entire passage is on media messages. Choice A is literally and contextually appropriate, and the reader can understand that the author would like to keep the introduction focused on the topic the passage is going to discuss.

12. A
This question tests a reader's inference skills. The extreme use of the word "all" in choice B suggests that every single advertising company are working to be approachable, and while this is not only unlikely, the text specifically states that "more" companies have done this, signifying that they have not all participated, even if it's a possibility that they may some day. The use of the limiting word "only" in choice C lends that answer similar problems; women are still buying from companies who do not care about this message, or those companies would not be in business, and the passage specifies that "many" women are worried about media messages, but not all. Readers may find choice D logical, especially if they are looking to make an inference, and while this may be a possibility, the passage does not suggest or discuss this happening. Choice A is correct based on specifically because of the relation between "still working" in the answer and "will hopefully" and the extensive discussion on companies struggles, which come only with progress, in the text.

13. C
This question tests the reader's summarization skills. The entire passage is leading up to the idea that the president of the US may not have had grounds to assert his Fourteen Points when other countries had lost so much. Choice A is pretty directly inferred by the text, but it does not adequately summarize what the entire passage is trying to communicate. Choice B may also be inferred by the passage when it says that the war is "imminent," but it does not represent the entire message, either. The passage does seem to be in praise of FDR, or at least in respect of him, but it does not in any way claim that he is the smartest president, nor does this represent the many other points included. Choice C is then the obvious answer, and most directly relates to the closing sentences which it rewords.

14. C
This question tests the reader's attention to detail. The passage does state that choices A and B are true, and while those statements are in proximity to the explanation for why the war started, they are not the reason given. Choice D is a mix up of words used in the passage, which says that the largest powers were in play but not that this fact somehow started the war. The passage does make a direct statement that a domino effect started the war, supporting choice C as the correct answer.

15. A
This question tests the reader's understanding of functions in writing. Throughout the passage, it states that leaders of other nations were hesitant to accept generous or peaceful terms because of the grievances of the war, and the great loss of life was chief among these. While the passage does touch on the devastation of deadly weapons (B), the use of this raw, emotional fact serves a much larger purpose, and the focus of the passage is not the weapons. While readers may indeed consider who lost the most soldiers (C) when, so many countries were involved and the inequalities of loss are mentioned in the passage, there is no discussion of this in the passage. Choice D is related to A, but choice A is more direct and relates more to the passage.

16. B
This question tests the reader's vocabulary skills. Choice A may seem appealing to readers because it is phonetically similar to "catalysed," but the two are not related in any other way. Choice C makes sense in context, but if plugged in to the sentence creates a redundancy that doesn't make sense. Choice D does also not make sense contextually, even if the reader may consider that funds were needed to create more weaponry, especially if it was advanced.

17. A
The correct order of ingredients is brown sugar, baking soda and chocolate chips.

18. B
Sturdy: strong, solid in structure or person. In context, Stir in chocolate chips by hand with a *sturdy* wooden spoon.

19. A
Disperse: to scatter in different directions or break up. In context, Stir until the chocolate chips and nuts are evenly *dispersed.*

20. B
You can stop stirring the nuts when they are evenly distributed. From the passage, "Stir until the chocolate chips and nuts are evenly dispersed."

21. B
The time limit for radar detectors is 14 days. Since you made the purchase 15 days ago, you do not qualify for the guarantee.

22. B
Since you made the purchase 10 days ago, you are covered by the guarantee. Since it is an advertised price at a different store, ABC Electric will "beat" the price by 10% of the difference, which is,

500 – 400 = 100 – difference in price

100 X 10% = $10 – 10% of the difference

The advertised lower price is $400. ABC will beat this price by 10% so they will refund $100 + 10 = $110.

23. C
The purpose of this passage is to persuade.

24. B
The correct answer can be found in the fourth sentence of the first paragraph.

Choice A is incorrect because repenting begins the day AFTER Mardi Gras. Choice C is incorrect because you can celebrate Mardi Gras without being a member of a Krewe.

Choice D is incorrect because exploration does not play any role in a modern Mardi Gras celebration.

25. A
The second sentence is the last paragraph states that Krewes are led by the Kings and Queens. Therefore, you must have to be part of a Krewe to be its King or its Queen.

Choice B is incorrect because it never states in the passage that only people from France can be Kings and Queen of Mardi Gras

Choice C is incorrect because the passage says nothing about having to speak French.

Choice D is incorrect because the passage does state that the Kings and Queens throw doubloons, which is fake money.

26. C
The first sentences of BOTH the 2nd and 3rd paragraphs mention that French explorers started this tradition in New Orleans.
Choices A, B and D are incorrect because they are names of cities or countries listed in the 2nd paragraph.

27. B
In the final paragraph, the word spectator is used to describe people who are watching the parade and catching cups, beads and doubloons.

Choices A and C are incorrect because we know the people who participate are part of Krewes. People who work the floats and parades are also part of Krewes

Choice D is incorrect because the passage makes no mention of people who do not celebrate Mardi Gras.

28. A
Caterpillars spend most of their time eating.

29. B
Some caterpillars are herbivores, others eat other insects (carnivores).

30. B
From the passage, the ants provide some degree of protection.

Section II – Number Operations

1. D
8327 – 1278 = 7049

2. B
294 X 21 = 6174

3. C
1278 + 4920 = 6198

4. A
285 * 12 = 3420

5. C
4120 – 3216 = 904

6. D
2417 + 1004 = 3421

7. B
1440 ÷ 12 = 120

8. C
2713 – 1308 = 1405

9. B
 (14 + 2) x 2 + 3 = 35

10. D
Original price = x,
80/100 = 12590/X,
80X = 1259000,
X = 15737.50.

11. A
25% = 25/100 = 1/4

12. A
143 * 4 = 572

13. C
125/100 = 1.25

14. C
$10^4 / 10^2 = 10^{4+2} = 10^6$

15. D
40/100 = 30/X = 40X = 30*100 = 3000/40 = 75

16. B
12.5/100 = 50/X = 12.5X = 50 * 100 = 5000/12.5 = 400

17. C
24/56 = 3/7 (divide numerator and denominator by 8)

18. C
Converting percent to decimal – divide percent by 100 and remove the % sign. 87% = 87/100 = .87

19. A
60 has the same relation to X as 75 to 100 – so
60/X = 75/100
6000 = 75X
X = 80

20. C
10 x 2 – (7 + 9) = 4

21. D
60 has the same relationship to 100 as 12 does to X – so
60/100 = 12/X
1200 = 60X
X = 20

22. C
Converting a fraction to a decimal – divide the numerator by the denominator – so 71/1000 = .071. Dividing by 1000 moves the decimal point 3 places.

23. C
3^3 = 81

24. C
4.7 + .9 + .01 = 5.61

25. A
.33 × .59 = .1947

26. C
11 + 19 x 2 = 49

27. D
.84 ÷ .7 = 1.2

28. C
9 is in the ten thousandths place in 1.7389.

29. A
.87 - .48 = .39

30. C
1 foot = 12 inches, 60 feet = 60 x 12 = 720 inches.

31. C

3/2 is the largest number.
Here are the choices:

    a. 1
    b. $\sqrt{2}$ = 1.414
    c. 3/2 = 1.5
    d. 4/3 = 1.33

32. A
465,890 - 456,890 = 9,000.

33. D
The jacket costs $545.00 so we can round up to $550. 10% of $550 is 55. We can round down to $50, which is easier to work with. $550 - $50 is $500. The jacket will cost about $500.

The actual cost will be 10% X 545 = $54.50
545 – 54.50 = $490.50

34. A
√121 = 11

35. C
√36 = 6

36. A
7 + 2 x (6 + 3) ÷ 3 - 7 = 16
For order of operation follow these rules:
Rule 1: Start with calculations that are inside brackets or parentheses.
Rule 2: Then, solve all multiplications and divisions, from left to right.
Rule 3: Finally, solve all additions and subtractions, from left to right.

37. D
1628 / 4 = 407

38. B
46 * 15 = 690

39. D
5575 + 8791 = 14,366

40. A
6149 / 143 = 43

Part III - Vocabulary

1. A
Verbiage NOUN speech with too many words.

2. A
Attache NOUN an aide or assistant.

3. A
Wreak VERB to cause or inflict especially related to harm or injury.

4. B
Witless ADJECTIVE foolish, without understanding.

5. A
Xenophobia NOUN a strong fear of strangers.

6. C
Zenith NOUN highest point, highest state, or peak,.

7. C
Zephyr NOUN light wind or gentle breeze.

8. A
Truism NOUN self-evident or clear obvious truth.

9. A
Ulterior ADJECTIVE beyond what is obvious or evident.

10. D
Vapid ADJECTIVE tasteless or bland.

11. B
Waif NOUN homeless child or stray.

12. B
Whine VERB Complaint or criticism.

13. C
Underling NOUN subordinate of lesser rank or authority.

14. A
Yearling NOUN a young animal that is between 1 and 2 years.

15. B
Verdure NOUN lush green vegetation.

16. B
Zealot NOUN a person who is very passionate and fanatic about his specific objectives or beliefs.

17. C
Vertigo NOUN dizziness.

18. B
Conspicuous ADJECTIVE obvious or easy to notice.

19. D
Benevolence NOUN disposition to do good.

20. A
Boisterous ADJECTIVE full of energy; exuberant; noisy.

21. B
Fondle VERB to touch or stroke.

22. A
Momentous ADJECTIVE outstanding in importance.

23. A
Antagonist NOUN an opponent or enemy.

24. B
Memento NOUN a keepsake; an object kept as a reminder of a place or event.

25. C
Insidious ADJECTIVE producing harm in a stealthy, often gradual, manner.

26. C
Itinerary NOUN a route or proposed route of a journey.

27. D
Illustrious ADJECTIVE dignified.

28. A
Mutation NOUN change or alteration.

29. B
Resent VERB to express displeasure or indignation.

30. A
Chubby ADJECTIVE fat, plump and overweight.

31. A
Skittish ADJECTIVE fearful or timid.

32. A
Rambunctious ADJECTIVE harsh or rough sounding.

33. C
Amphibious ADJECTIVE living both on land and in water.

34. B
Nuance NOUN a slight degree of difference in anything perceptible to the sense of the mind.

35. A
Contempt NOUN The feeling that a person or thing is beneath consideration, worthless, or deserving of scorn.

36. A
Heresy NOUN Belief or opinion contrary to orthodox religious beliefs

37. D
Temperance (noun) Abstinence from alcoholic drink.

38. B
Hyperbole NOUN Exaggerated claims or statements not intended to be taken literally.

39. B
Connotation NOUN An idea or meaning suggested by or associated with a word or thing:

40. B
Penultimate ADJECTIVE Second to last.

CRACKING THE CODE
HOW TO BUILD YOUR
VOCABULARY

If you've ever looked at a long list of words and felt like you were trying to memorize a phone book, I've got good news for you: there's a much better way. In my years helping folks get ready for the CAAT, I've found that the most successful students don't just "memorize"—they "investigate."

Think of English words like a set of Lego blocks. Most of the "big" words that look intimidating at first are actually just smaller, familiar pieces snapped together. Once you learn how to spot those pieces, you won't need to carry a dictionary in your head; you'll be able to figure out the meaning of a word you've never even seen before.

In this chapter, we're going to give you the "toolbox" to take these words apart. Here is what we're going to cover:

> **Prefixes and Suffixes:** We'll look at the "attachments" added to the beginning and ends of words that change their direction or meaning.

> **The Heart of the Word (Roots):** I've put together an extensive list of Latin and Greek roots. If you know the

root, you know the "family" the word belongs to.

Meaning in Context: Sometimes, a word is a "double agent" with two different meanings. We'll practice how to use the surrounding sentences as clues to figure out which job the word is doing.

Hands-on Practice: After each section, I've included practice questions. It's one thing to read about it at the kitchen table; it's another to put those tools to work!

Don't Swallow the Ocean

You don't need to master this whole chapter in one afternoon. Take it one "piece" at a time. Maybe spend today on prefixes, and tomorrow on a few root words. Vocabulary is like a muscle—you build it with small, daily workouts, not one giant lift.

Vocabulary - Unlocking Big Ideas
Meaning in Context Answer Sheet

1. A B C D
2. A B C D
3. A B C D
4. A B C D
5. A B C D
6. A B C D
7. A B C D
8. A B C D
9. A B C D
10. A B C D
11. A B C D
12. A B C D
13. A B C D
14. A B C D
15. A B C D
16. A B C D
17. A B C D
18. A B C D
19. A B C D
20. A B C D
21. A B C D
22. A B C D
23. A B C D
24. A B C D
25. A B C D
26. A B C D
27. A B C D
28. A B C D
29. A B C D
30. A B C D
31. A B C D
32. A B C D
33. A B C D
34. A B C D
35. A B C D
36. A B C D
37. A B C D
38. A B C D
39. A B C D
40. A B C D

Meaning in Context

Meaning in context is a powerful tool for learning vocabulary. You make an educated guess of the meaning from the context of the sentence. With meaning in context questions, also called sentence completion, you don't have to know the exact meaning - just an approximate meaning to answer the question.

This is also true is when reading. Sometimes it is necessary to know the exact meaning. Other times, the exact meaning is not important and you can make an educated guess from the context and continue reading.

The meaning in context exercises below give you practice making guesses about the meaning.

Directions: For each of the questions below, choose the word with the meaning best suited to the sentence based on the context.

1. When Joe broke his _____ in a skiing accident, his entire leg was in a cast.

    a. Ankle

    b. Humerus

    c. Wrist

    d. Femur

2. Alan had to learn the _____ system of numbering when his family moved to Great Britain.

    a. American

    b. Decimal

    c. Metric

    d. Fingers and toes

VOCABULARY- UNLOCKING BIG IDEAS

3. After Lisa's aunt had her tenth child, Lisa found that she had more than twenty _____.

   a. Uncles
   b. Friends
   c. Stepsisters
   d. Cousins

4. Although he had flown many times, this was his first flight in a _____.

   a. Helicopter
   b. Kite
   c. Train
   d. Subway car

5. George is very serious about his _____, and recently joined the American Scholastic Association.

   a. Schoolwork
   b. Cooking
   c. Travelling
   d. Athletics

6. She was a rabid Red Sox fan, attending every game, and demonstrating her _____ by cheering more loudly than anyone else.

   a. Knowledge
   b. Boredom
   c. Commitment
   d. Enthusiasm

7. When Craig's dog was struck by a car, he rushed his pet to the _____.

    a. Emergency room

    b. Doctor

    c. Veterinarian

    d. Podiatrist

8. After she received her influenza vaccination, Nan thought that she was _____ to the common cold.

    a. Immune

    b. Susceptible

    c. Vulnerable

    d. At risk

9. Paul's rose bushes were being destroyed by Japanese beetles, so he invested in a good _____.

    a. Fungicide

    b. Fertilizer

    c. Sprinkler

    d. Pesticide

10. The last time that the crops failed, the entire nation experienced months of _____.

    a. Famine

    b. Harvest

    c. Plenitude

    d. Disease

Vocabulary - Unlocking Big Ideas

11. Because of a pituitary dysfunction, Karl lacked the necessary _____ to grow as tall as his father.

    a. Glands

    b. Hormones

    c. Vitamins

    d. Testosterone

12. Because of its colorful fall _____ , the maple is my favorite tree.

    a. Growth

    b. Branches

    c. Greenery

    d. Foliage

13. When Mr. Davis returned from southern Asia, he told us about the _____ that sometimes swept the area, bringing torrential rain.

    a. Monsoons

    b. Hurricanes

    c. Blizzards

    d. Floods

14. Is it true that _____ always grows on the north side of trees?

    a. Grass

    b. Moss

    c. Ferns

    d. Ground cover

15. You can _____ some fires by covering them with dirt, while others require foam or water.

    a. Extinguish
    b. Distinguish
    c. Ignite
    d. Lessen

16. Through powerful fans that circulate the heat over the food, _____ ovens work very efficiently.

    a. Microwave
    b. Broiler
    c. Convection
    d. Pressure

17. Because of the growing use of _____ as a fuel, corn production has greatly increased.

    a. Alcohol
    b. Ethanol
    c. Natural gas
    d. Oil

18. In heavily industrialized areas, the air pollution causes many _____ diseases.

    a. Respiratory
    b. Cardiac
    c. Alimentary
    d. Circulatory

19. Because hydroelectric power is a _____ source of energy, its use is considered a green energy.

   a. Significant
   b. Disposable
   c. Renewable
   d. Reusable

20. The process required the use of highly _____ liquids, so fire extinguishers were everywhere in the factory.

   a. Erratic
   b. Combustible
   c. Inflammable
   d. Neutral

21. I still don't know exactly. That isn't _____ evidence.

   a. Undeterred
   b. Unrelenting
   c. Unfortunate
   d. Conclusive

22. He could manipulate the coins in his fingers very _____.

   a. Brazenly
   b. Eloquently
   c. Boisterously
   d. Deftly

23. His investment scheme _____ many serious investors, who lost money.

   a. Helped
   b. Vindicated
   c. Duped
   d. Reproved

24. When we go to a party, we always _____ a driver.

   a. Feign
   b. Exploit
   c. Dote
   d. Designate

25. This new evidence should _____ any doubts.

   a. Dispel
   b. Dispense
   c. Evaluate
   d. Diverse

26. She went to Asia on $10 a day – her _____ travelling plans are amazing.

   a. Frothy
   b. Frugal
   c. Fraught
   d. Focal

VOCABULARY- UNLOCKING BIG IDEAS

27. My grandmother's house is full or trinkets and ornaments. She is always buying _____.

   a. Collectibles

   b. Baubles

   c. China

   d. Crystal

28. I am finally out of debt! I paid off all of my _____.

   a. Debtors

   b. Defendants

   c. Accounts Receivable

   d. Creditors

29. I love listening to his speeches. He has a gift for _____.

   a. Oratory

   b. Irony

   c. Jargon

   d. None of the above

30. The warehouse went bankrupt so all the furniture has to be _____.

   a. Dissected

   b. Liquidated

   c. Destroyed

   d. Bought

31. He sold the property when he didn't even own it. The whole thing was a _____.

   a. Hoax
   b. Feign
   c. Defile
   d. Default

32. The repair really isn't working. Those parts you replaced are _____.

   a. Despondent
   b. Illusive
   c. Deficient
   d. Granular

33. Just because she is supervisor, doesn't mean we have to _____ in front of her.

   a. Foible
   b. Grovel
   c. Humiliate
   d. Indispose

34. That noise is _____ ! It is driving me crazy.

   a. Loud
   b. Intolerable
   c. Frivolous
   d. Fictitious

Vocabulary- Unlocking Big Ideas

35. Her inheritance was a good size and included many _____.

    a. Heirlooms
    b. Perchance
    c. Cynical
    d. Lateral

36. I see that sign everywhere. It is much more _____ than I thought.

    a. Prelude
    b. Prevalent
    c. Ratify
    d. Rational

37. Her attitude was very casual and _____.

    a. Idle
    b. Nonchalant
    c. Portly
    d. Portend

38. The machine _____ the rock into ore.

    a. Quells
    b. Pulverizes
    c. Eradicates
    d. Segments

39. The water in the pond has been sitting for so long it is _____.

    a. Stagnant
    b. Sediment
    c. Stupor
    d. Residue

40. She didn't listen to a thing and _____ all the objections.

    a. Manipulated
    b. Mired
    c. Furtive
    d. Rebuffed

Vocabulary- Unlocking Big Ideas

Answer Key

1. D
Femur NOUN A thighbone.

2. C
Metric System a system of measurements that is based on the base units of the meter/metre, the kilogram, the second, the ampere, the kelvin, the mole, and the candela.

3. D
Cousins NOUN the son or daughter of a person's uncle or aunt; a first cousin.

4. A
Helicopter

5. A
Schoolwork

6. D
Enthusiasm NOUN intensity of feeling; excited interest or eagerness.

7. C
Veterinarian NOUN medical doctor who treats non-human animals.

8. A
Immune ADJECTIVE protected by inoculation, or due to innate resistance to pathogens.

9. D
Pesticide NOUN a substance, usually synthetic although sometimes biological, used to kill or contain the activities of pests.

10. A
Famine NOUN a period of extreme shortage of food in a region.

11. B
Hormones NOUN any substance produced by one tissue and conveyed by the bloodstream to another to effect physiological activity.

12. D
Foliage NOUN the leaves of plants.

13. A
Monsoons NOUN tropical rainy season when the rain lasts for several months with few interruptions.

14. B
Moss NOUN any of various small green plants growing on the ground or on the surfaces of trees, stones etc.

15. A
Extinguish NOUN to put out, as in fire; to end burning; to quench.

16. C
Convection NOUN the vertical movement of heat and moisture.

17. B
Ethanol NOUN a type of alcohol used as fuel.

18. A
Respiratory NOUN relating to respiration; breathing.

19. D
Reusable NOUN able to be used again; especially after salvaging or special treatment or processing.

20. B
Combustible NOUN capable of burning.

21. D
Conclusive ADJECTIVE providing an end to something; decisive.

22. D
Deftly ADVERB quickly and neatly in action.

23. C
Dupe VERB to swindle, deceive, or trick.

24. D
Designate ADJECTIVE appointed; chosen.

25. A
Dispel VERB to drive away by scattering, or so to cause to vanish; to clear away.

26. B
Frugal ADJECTIVE cheap, economical, thrifty.

27. B
Baubles NOUN a cheap showy ornament.

28. D
Creditors NOUN a person to whom a debt is owed.

29. A
Oratory NOUN the art of public speaking, especially in a formal, expressive, or forceful manner.

30. B
Liquidate VERB to convert assets into cash.

31. A
Hoax NOUN to deceive (someone) by making them believe something which has been maliciously or mischievously fabricated.

32. C
Deficient ADJECTIVE lacking something essential.

33. B
Grovel VERB to abase oneself before another person.

34. B
Intolerable ADJECTIVE not capable of being borne or endured; not proper or right to be allowed; insufferable; insupportable; unbearable.

35. A
Heirloom NOUN A valued possession that has been passed down through the generations.

36. B
Prevalent ADJECTIVE Widespread.

37. B
Nonchalant ADJECTIVE Casually calm and relaxed.

38. B
Pulverizes VERB to completely destroy, especially by crushing to fragments or a powder.

39. A
Stagnant ADJECTIVE lacking freshness, motion, flow, progress, or change; stale; motionless; still.

40. D
Rebuff NOUN a sudden resistance or refusal.

Vocabulary- Unlocking Big Ideas
Top 100 Common Vocabulary

Learning vocabulary, especially in a hurry for an exam, means that you will be making friends with a lot of different word lists. Below is a word list of top 100 "must know" vocabulary to get you started.

When studying word lists, think of different ways to mix-it-up. Work with a friend or a study group and compare word lists and test each other, or make flash cards.

1. **Abate** VERB reduce or lesson.
2. **Abandon** VERB to give up completely.
3. **Aberration** NOUN something unusual, different from the norm.
4. **Abet** VERB to encourage or support.
5. **Abstain** VERB to refrain from doing something.
6. **Abrogate** VERB to abolish or render void.
7. **Aesthetic** ADJECTIVE pertaining to beauty.
8. **Abstemious** ADJECTIVE moderate in the use of food or drink.
9. **Anachronistic** ADJECTIVE out of the context of time, out of date.
10. **Acrimonious** ADJECTIVE sharp or harsh in language or temper.
11. **Asylum** NOUN sanctuary, place of safety.
12. **Banal** ADJECTIVE lacking in freshness, originality, or vigor.
13. **Bias** NOUN a prejudice towards something or against something.
14. **Belie** VERB to give a false idea of.
15. **Brazen** ADJECTIVE bold.
16. **Belligerent** ADJECTIVE engaged in war.
17. **Camaraderie** NOUN togetherness, trust, group dynamic of trust.
18. **Cabal** NOUN a small group of persons engaged in plotting.
19. **Capacious** ADJECTIVE very large, spacious.
20. **Callous** ADJECTIVE unfeeling or insensitive.
21. **Clairvoyant** ADJECTIVE can predict the future.

22. **Cantankerous** ADJECTIVE ill-natured; quarrelsome.
23. **Compassion** NOUN sympathy.
24. **Capricious** ADJECTIVE quick to find fault about trifles.
25. **Condescending** ADJECTIVE patronizing.
26. **Chauvinist** NOUN an extreme patriot.
27. **Conformist** NOUN someone who follows the majority.
28. **Clamorous** VERB loud and noisy.
29. **Deleterious** ADJECTIVE harmful.
30. **Deference** NOUN submitting to the wishes or judgment of another.
31. **Digression** NOUN straying from main point.
32. **Delectable** ADJECTIVE very pleasing.
33. **Discredit** NOUN dishonor someone, prove something untrue.
34. **Demeanor** NOUN behavior; bearing.
35. **Divergent** ADJECTIVE moving apart, going in different directions.
36. **Edict** NOUN a public command or proclamation issued by an authority.
37. **Emulate** NOUN following someone else's example.
38. **Effete** ADJECTIVE no longer productive; hence, lacking in or, worn out.
39. **Ephemeral** ADJECTIVE fleeting, temporary.
40. **Elicit** VERB to draw out.
41. **Exemplary** ADJECTIVE outstanding.
42. **Elucidate** VERB to make clear; to explain florid: ornate.
43. **Forbearance** NOUN patience, restraint.
44. **Facade** NOUN front or face, especially of a building.
45. **Fortuitous** ADJECTIVE lucky.
46. **Fallacious** ADJECTIVE unsound; misleading; deceptive.
47. **Fraught** NOUN filled with or likely to result in (some thing undesirable).
48. **Flaccid** ADJECTIVE lacking firmness.
49. **Ghastly** ADJECTIVE horrible, deathlike.
50. **Grimace** NOUN a distortion of the face to express an attitude or feeling.
51. **Hedonist** NOUN person who acts in pursuit of pleasure.
52. **Harbinger** NOUN a forerunner; ail announcer.

Vocabulary- Unlocking Big Ideas

53. **Impetuous** ADJECTIVE rash, impulsive.
54. **Immaculate** ADJECTIVE spotless; pure.
55. **Inconsequential** ADJECTIVE without consequence, trivial, does not matter.
56. **Impeccable** ADJECTIVE faultless.
57. **Intrepid** ADJECTIVE fearless.
58. **Imprecation** NOUN a curse.
59. **Jubilation** NOUN extreme happiness, joy.
60. **Latent** ADJECTIVE hidden; present but not fully developed.
61. **Longevity** NOUN long (particularly long life).
62. **Maudlin** ADJECTIVE sentimental to the point of tears.
63. **Nonchalant** ADJECTIVE casual, calm, at ease.
64. **Oblivious** ADJECTIVE forgetful; absent-minded.
65. **Orator** NOUN speaker.
66. **Obviate** VERB to prevent, dispose of, or make un necessary by appropriate actions.
67. **Parched** ADJECTIVE lacking water, dried up.
68. **Panacea** NOUN a remedy for all ills.
69. **Pragmatic** ADJECTIVE practical.
70. **Paraphrase** VERB to restate the meaning of a passage in other words.
71. **Pretentious** ADJECTIVE being self important, thinking you are better than others.
72. **Pecuniary** ADJECTIVE pertaining to money.
73. **Prosaic** ADJECTIVE ordinary.
74. **Pensive** ADJECTIVE sadly thoughtful.
75. **Provocative** ADJECTIVE causes a fuss, inflammatory, likely to get people riled up.
76. **Peruse** VERB to read carefully.
77. **Querulous** ADJECTIVE irritable, prone to argument.
78. **Radical** NOUN one who advocates extreme basic changes.
79. **Reclusive** ADJECTIVE hermit, withdrawn.
80. **Recapitulate** VERB to restate in a brief, concise form.
81. **Renovate** VERB to make new, being redone.
82. **Refute** VERB to prove incorrect or false.
83. **Reverence** NOUN deep respect.
84. **Sallow** ADJECTIVE sick.
85. **Scrutinize** VERB to look at carefully.
86. **Sanguinary** ADJECTIVE bloody.

87. **Spurious** ADJECTIVE false, untrue.
88. **Scourge** VERB to punish severely; to afflict; to whip.
89. **Substantiate** VERB to confirm, prove.
90. **Scrutinize** VERB to examine carefully.
91. **Superficial** ADJECTIVE shallow.
92. **Sleazy** ADJECTIVE flimsy and cheap.
93. **Surreptitious** ADJECTIVE secret.
94. **Tactful** ADJECTIVE polite.
95. **Tangible** ADJECTIVE real; actual.
96. **Transient** ADJECTIVE temporary, impermanent.
97. **Vanquish** VERB to subdue or conquer.
98. **Vindicate** VERB to free from blame.
99. **Wary** ADJECTIVE careful, watchful.
100. **Zenith** NOUN the highest point.

Vocabulary - Unlocking Big Ideas

Stem Words

Probably the best way of learning new vocabulary is our "two-for-one" strategy of learning a stem word and then you can recognize two, three or more words that use the stem word. If you are studying for an exam with a vocabulary section, this is the best strategy for you.

Below is an extensive list of stem words with their meaning and examples, followed by questions

A Root	Meaning	Examples
ab-, a-, abs-	away	absent, aversion
acr(i)-	sharp, pungent	acrid, acrimony
aer-, aero-	air, atmosphere	aeronautics, aerosol
agri-	field, country	agriculture,
amic-, imic-	friend	amicable, inimical
ant-, anti-	against, opposed to, preventive	antibiotic, antipodes
ante-, anti-	before, in front of, prior to	anticipate, antiquarian
anthropo-	human	anthropology, anthropomorphic
aqu-	water	aquarium, aqueduct
arche-, archi-	ruler	archangel, archetype
archaeo-, archeo-	ancient	archeology, archaic
arthr(o)-	joint	arthritis, arthropod
astr-, astro-	star, star-shaped	asterisk, astronomy
aud(i)-	hearing, listening, sound	auditorium, auditory
aut-, auto-	self; directed from within	automobile, autonomy
avi-	bird	aviary, aviation

B Root	Meaning	Example #1
baro-	weight, pressure	barometer, barograph
basi-	at the bottom	basic, basis
bell(i)-	war	bellicose, belligerent
bibl-	book	bibliography, bible
bi(o)-	life	biology, biosphere
brev(i)-	brief, short (time)	abbreviation, brevity

C Root	Meaning	Examples
cand-	glowing, iridescent	incandescent, candle
cap-, -cip-, capt-, -cept-	hold, take	capture, recipient
cardi(o)-	relating to the heart	cardiology, cardiograph
cav-	hollow	cavity, excavation
cent-	hundred	centennial, centurion
chloro-	green	chlorine, chlorophyll,
chron-	time	chronometer, chronology
circum-	around	circumference, circumcise
clar-	clear	clarity, declaration
clin-	bed, lean	Recline, inclined
cogn-	know	cognitive, recognize
contra-	against	contrast, contradict
cre-	make	creation, creature
cred-	believe, trust	credibility, credentials
cruc(i)-	cross	crucifix, crucify
crypt-	hidden	cryptic, cryptography

curr-, curs-	run	concurrent, recursion
cycl(o)-	circular	bicycle, cycle, cyclone

D Root	Meaning	Examples
de-	from, away from, removing	delete, demented
dens-	thick	condense, density
dent-	tooth	dental, dentures
	skin	dermis, epidermis
dorm-	sleep	dormant, dormitory

E Root	Meaning	Examples
equ-, -iqu-	even, level	equal, equivalence
ethn-	native	ethnicity, ethnic
eu-	well, good	euphoria, euthanasia
ex-, e-, ef-	from, out	exclude, extrude, extend
exter-, extra-	outer	exterior, extrasensory
extrem-	utmost, outermost	extremity, extremophile

G Root	Meaning	Examples
ger-, gest-	bear, carry	digest, gestation
glob-	sphere	global, globule
grad-, gress-	walk, step	grade, regress
gran-	grain	granary, granule
greg-	flock	gregarious, segregation

H Root	Meaning	Examples
haem-	blood	haemophilia, haemoglobin
hemi-	half	hemicycle, hemisphere
her-, hes-	cling	adhesive, coherent
hom(o)-	same	homosexual, homogenous
hort(i)-	garden	horticulture, horticulturist
hospit-	host	hospitality, hospitable
hydr(o)-	water	hydrophobia, hydroponic

I Root	Meaning	Examples
idi(o)-	personal	idiom, idiosyncrasy
ign-	fire	igneous, ignition
infra-	below, under	infrastructure, infrared
inter-	among, between	intermission, intersection

J Root	Meaning	Examples
jac- -ject-	cast, throw	eject, interject
jung-, junct-	join	conjunction, juncture
juven-	young, youth	juvenile, rejuvenate

K Root	Meaning	Examples
kil(o)-	thousand	kilobyte, kilogram, kilometer
kine-	movement, motion	Kinetic, kinesthetic

VOCABULARY- UNLOCKING BIG IDEAS

L Root	Meaning	Examples
lab-, laps-	slide, slip	elapse, relapse
lact-	milk	lactate, lactose
lax-	not tense	laxative, relaxation
leg-	law	legal, legislative
lev-	lift, light	elevator, levitation
liber-	free	liberation, liberty
lingu-	language, tongue	bilingual, linguistic
loc-	place	local, location
long-	long	elongate, longitude
lumin-	light	illumination, luminous
lun-	moon	lunar, lunatic

M Root	Meaning	Examples
maj-	greater	majesty, majority
mal-	bad	malicious, malignant
mania	mental illness	kleptomania, maniac
manu-	hand	manual, manuscript
mar-	sea	marine, maritime
maxim-	greatest	maximal, maximum
medi-, -midi-	middle	median, medieval
ment-	mind	demented, mentality
merc-	reward, wages	mercantile, merchant
merg-, mers-	dip, plunge	emerge, immersion
meter-, metr-	measure	metric, thermometer
micr(o)-	small	microphone, microscope
migr-	wander	emigrant, migrate
milit-	soldier	military, militia
mill-	thousand	millennium, million
mim-	repeat	mime, mimic
min-	less, smaller	minority, minuscule
mir-	wonder, amazement	admire, miracle
misce-, mixt-	mix	miscellaneous, mixture
mitt-, miss-	send	intermittent, transmission

M con't		
mon(o)-	one	monolith, monotone
mort-	death	immortal, mortuary
mov-, mot-	move	motion, momentum
mult(i)-	many, much	multiple, multiplex

N Root	Meaning	Examples
narc-	numb	narcosis, narcotic
nav-	ship	naval, navigate
neur-	nerve	neurology, neurosurgeon
nud-	naked	denude, nude
nutri	nourish	nutrition, nutrient

O Root	Meaning	Examples
ob-, o-, oc-, os-	against	obstinate, ostentatious
oct-	eight	octagon, octahedron
ocul-	eye	ocular, oculus
omni-	all	omnipotence, omnivore
opt-	eye	optical, optician
opt-	choose	adopt, optional
or-	mouth	oral, orator
ordin-	order	ordinal, ordinary
orn-	decorate	adorn, ornament
ov-	egg	oval, ovule

P Root	Meaning	Examples
pac-	peace	pacifism, pacifist
paed-, ped	child	pediatric, pediatrician
pall-	be pale	pallid, pallor
pand-, pans-	spread	expand, expansion
par(a)-	beside, near	parallel, parameter
past-	feed	pasture, repast
ped-	foot, child	pedal, quadruped
pharmac-	drug, medicine	pharmacy, pharmacist

P con't		
phob-	fear	hydrophobia, agoraphobia
phon(o)-	sound	microphone, phonograph
plan-	flat	planar, plane
plas-	mould	plasma, plastic
plaus-	clap	applaud, applause
pod-	foot	podiatry, tripod
pol-	pole	dipole, polar
pole-, poli-	city	metropolis, politics
port-	carry	export, transportation
post-	after, behind	posterior, postscript
pre-	before	prehistoric, previous
prim-	first	primary, primeval
priv(i)-	separate	deprivation, privilege
proxim-	nearest	approximate, proximity
pugn-	fight	pugnacious, repugnant

Q Root	Meaning	Examples
quadr-	four	quadrangle, quadrillion
quin-	fifth	quintary, quintile
quot-	how many, how great	quota, quotient

R Root	Meaning	Examples
rad-, ras-	scrape, shave	abrade, abrasion
ranc-	rancidness, grudge, bitterness	rancid, rancour
re-, red-	again, back	recede, redact
retro-	backward, behind	retrograde, retrospective

R con't		
rid-, ris-	laugh	derision, ridicule
rod-, ros-	gnaw	erosion, rodent
rump-, rupt-	break	eruption, rupture

S Root	Meaning	Examples
sacr-, secr-	sacred	consecrate, sacrament
sanc-	holy	sanctify, sanctuary
sci-	know	prescient, science
scind-, sciss-	split	rescind, scissors
scrib-, script-	write	inscribe, scripture
se-, sed-	apart	secede, sedition
sect-, seg-	cut	section, segment
sed-	settle, calm	sedative, sedate
sema-	sign	semantics, semaphore
sen-	old man	senator, senility
sequ-, secut-	follow	consecutive, sequence
sign-	sign	design, designate
sist-	cause to stand	consist, persistence
soci-	group	associate, social
sol-	sun	solar
sol-	comfort	soothe, consolation
sol-	alone, only	sole, solo
solv-, solut-	loosen, set free	dissolve, solution
sorb-, sorpt-	suck	absorb, absorption
spec-, -spic-, spect-	look	conspicuous, inspection, specimen
spher-	ball	sphere, spheroid
squal-	scaly, dirty, filthy	squalid, squalor
statu-, -stitu-	stand	institution, statute
stell-	star	constellation, stellar
still-	drip	distillation
stinct-	apart	distinction, distinguish

S con't		
stru-, struct-	structure, building	construction, construe
subter-	under	subterfuge, subterranean
sum-, sumpt-	take	assumption, consume

T Root	Meaning	Examples
tac-, -tic-	be silent	reticent, tacit
tang-, -ting-, tact-, tag-	touch	contact, tactile
tele-	far, end	telegram, telephone
tempor-	time	contemporary, temporal
ten-, -tin-, tent-	hold	detention, tenacious
tend-, tens-	stretch	extend, extension
termin-	boundary, limit, end	terminal, termination
terr-	dry land	terrace, terrain
test-	witness	testament, testimony
tex-, text-	weave	texture, textile
tot-	all, whole	total, totality
trans-, tra-, tran-	across	tradition, transportation
traum-	wound	trauma, traumatic
tri-	three	triad, tripod
tri-	three	triangle, trivia
typ-	stamp, model	archetype, typography

U Root	Meaning	Examples
ultim-	farthest	ultimatum, ultimate
ut-, us-	use	usual, utility

V Root	Meaning	Examples
vac-	empty	vacancy, vacuum
vad-, vas-	go	evade, pervasive
vag-	wander	vague, vagabond
vap-	lack (of)	evaporation, vapid
ven-, vent-	come	advent, convention
vend-	sell	vendor, vending
verb-	word	verbal, verbatim
vert-, vers-	turn	convert, invert
veter-	old	inveterate, veteran
vi-	way	deviate, via
vid-, vis-	see	video, vision
vil-	cheap	vile, vilify
vinc-, vict-	conquer	invincible, victory
viv-	live	revive, survive, vivid
voc-	voice	vocal, provocative
volv-, volut-	roll	convolution, revolve
vor-, vorac-	swallow	devour, voracious

Z Root	Meaning	Examples
zo-	animal, living being	zoo, zoology

Vocabulary – Unlocking Big Ideas

Answer Sheet

	A	B	C	D	E		A	B	C	D	E
1	○	○	○	○	○	21	○	○	○	○	○
2	○	○	○	○	○	22	○	○	○	○	○
3	○	○	○	○	○	23	○	○	○	○	○
4	○	○	○	○	○	24	○	○	○	○	○
5	○	○	○	○	○	25	○	○	○	○	○
6	○	○	○	○	○						
7	○	○	○	○	○						
8	○	○	○	○	○						
9	○	○	○	○	○						
10	○	○	○	○	○						
11	○	○	○	○	○						
12	○	○	○	○	○						
13	○	○	○	○	○						
14	○	○	○	○	○						
15	○	○	○	○	○						
16	○	○	○	○	○						
17	○	○	○	○	○						
18	○	○	○	○	○						
19	○	○	○	○	○						
20	○	○	○	○	○						

Stem Words Practice Questions

1. Choose the meaning of the stem word quot-

   a. How many

   b. Development

   c. Field

   d. Government

2. Choose the meaning of the stem word stu-

   a. Health study

   b. Building

   c. Stretched out

   d. On both sides

3. Choose the meaning of the stem word baro-

   a. Weight or pressure

   b. North

   c. Brief

   d. Greatness

4. Choose the meaning of the stem word bibl-

   a. At the bottom

   b. Deep

   c. Book

   d. Wood

Vocabulary- Unlocking Big Ideas

5. Choose the meaning of the stem word vac-

    a. Pretty

    b. Stone

    c. Empty

    d. Vault

6. Choose the meaning of the stem word cand-

    a. Long

    b. Goat like

    c. Harden

    d. Glowing

7. Choose the meaning of the stem word temin-

    a. End

    b. Tenth part

    c. Leadership

    d. Move away from

8. Choose the meaning of the stem word derm-

    a. Above

    b. Skin

    c. Insane actions

    d. Fingers

9. Choose the meaning of the stem word equ-

    a. Even or level

    b. Knowledge

    c. Inside or within

    d. House

10. Choose the meaning of the stem word haem-

 a. Mental state

 b. Blood

 c. Child health

 d. Time

11. Choose the meaning of the stem word hemi-

 a. Half

 b. Air

 c. Strange

 d. Foreign

12. Choose the meaning of the stem word infra-

 a. Doubtful

 b. Foundation

 c. Strength

 d. Below or under

13. Choose the meaning of the stem word junct-

 a. Sound

 b. Join

 c. Jungle

 d. Electricity

14. Choose the meaning of the stem word lact-

 a. Shine

 b. Milk

 c. Lecture

 d. Teaching

VOCABULARY- UNLOCKING BIG IDEAS

15. Choose the meaning of the stem word lingu-

   a. Teacher

   b. Language, tongue

   c. Knowledge

   d. Tribes

16. Choose the meaning of the stem word nav-

   a. Slime

   b. Ship

   c. Join

   d. Tell

17. Choose the meaning of the stem word pac-

   a. Feed

   b. Ancient

   c. Peace

   d. Maiden

18. Choose the meaning of the stem word retro-

   a. Backward or behind

   b. Air less

   c. Kidney

   d. Nose or snout

19. Choose the meaning of the stem word rupt-

   a. Gnaw

   b. Prow

   c. Throat

   d. Break

20. Choose the meaning of the stem word sacr-

   a. Sacred
   b. Flesh
   c. Scratch
   d. Seriousness

21. Choose the meaning of the stem word termin-

   a. God
   b. Machine
   c. Boundary or end
   d. Weave

22. Choose the meaning of the stem word ultim-

   a. Fruitful
   b. Farthest
   c. Infection
   d. Shadow

23. Choose the meaning of the stem word ten-

   a. Sacred
   b. Flesh
   c. Scratch
   d. Hold

24. Choose the meaning of the stem word vi-

   a. God
   b. Way
   c. Boundary or end
   d. Weave

25. Choose the meaning of the stem word privi-

   a. Fruitful
   b. Farthest
   c. Infection
   d. Separate

Answer Key – Part I

1. A
The stem word quot- means how many, for example quota.

2. B
The stem word stu- means building, for example construction.

3. A
The stem word baro- means relating to weight or pressure, for example barometer.

4. C
The stem word bibl- relates to books, for example bibliography and bible.

5. C
The stem word vac- means empty, for example vacancy.

6. D
The stem word cand- means glowing, for examples candle and candid.

7. A
The stem word termin- means end, for example terminal.

8. B
The stem word derm- relates to skin, for example dermis and epidermis.

9. A
The stem word equ- means even or level, for example equal.

10. B
The stem word haem- means blood, for example hemophilia.

11. A
The stem word hemi- means half, for example hemisphere.

12. D
The stem word infra- means below and under, for example

VOCABULARY- UNLOCKING BIG IDEAS

infrastructure.

13. B
The stem word junct- means join, for example junction.

14. B
The stem word lact- means milk, for example lactate.

15. B
The stem word lingu- means relating to language, tongue, for example bilingual and linguistic.

16. B
The stem word nav- means ship, for example naval.

17. C
The stem word pac- means peace, for example pact and pacify.

18. A
The stem word retro- means backward or behind, for example retrospect and retrograde.

19. D
The stem word rupt- means break, for example rupture.

20. A
The stem word sacr- means sacred, for example consecrate and sacrament.

21. C
The stem word termin- means boundary or end, for examples termination and terminal.

22. B
The stem word ultim- means farthest, for example ultimate.

23. D
The stem word ten- means hold, for example detention.

24. B
The stem word vi- means way, for example via.

25. D
The stem word privi- means separate, for example privilege.

PASS THE CAAT!

Answer Sheet

	A	B	C	D	E		A	B	C	D	E
1	○	○	○	○	○	21	○	○	○	○	○
2	○	○	○	○	○	22	○	○	○	○	○
3	○	○	○	○	○	23	○	○	○	○	○
4	○	○	○	○	○	24	○	○	○	○	○
5	○	○	○	○	○	25	○	○	○	○	○
6	○	○	○	○	○						
7	○	○	○	○	○						
8	○	○	○	○	○						
9	○	○	○	○	○						
10	○	○	○	○	○						
11	○	○	○	○	○						
12	○	○	○	○	○						
13	○	○	○	○	○						
14	○	○	○	○	○						
15	○	○	○	○	○						
16	○	○	○	○	○						
17	○	○	○	○	○						
18	○	○	○	○	○						
19	○	○	○	○	○						
20	○	○	○	○	○						

VOCABULARY- UNLOCKING BIG IDEAS
Stem Words Practice Part II

1. Choose the stem word that means air or atmosphere.

    a. Bran-

    b. Gen-

    c. Aero-

    d. Agog-

2. Choose the stem word that means women, female.

    a. Fam-

    b. Ward-

    c. Gust-

    d. Femin-

3. Choose the stem word that means end.

    a. Gran-

    b. Fin-

    c. Flux-

    d. Eur-

4. Choose the stem word that means life.

    a. Bio-

    b. Calcu-

    c. Ext-

    d. Ago-

5. Choose the stem word that means outermost, utmost.

    a. Frug-

    b. Etym-

    c. Larg-

    d. Extrem-

6. Choose the stem word that means at the bottom.

    a. Trid-

    b. Eco-

    c. Basi-

    d. Ful-

7. Choose the stem word that means host.

    a. Hospit-

    b. Habi-

    c. Proc-

    d. Paci-

8. Choose the stem word that means people, race, tribe, nation.

    a. Adul-

    b. Baro-

    c. Cad-

    d. Ethn-

9. Choose the stem word that means idea; thought.

    a. Cupl(u)-

    b. Stat-

    c. Ide(o)-

    d. Anal-

Vocabulary- Unlocking Big Ideas

10. Choose the stem word that means among, between.

   a. Chang-

   b. Sta-

   c. Inter-

   d. Less-

11. Choose the stem word that means young, youth.

   a. Juven-

   b. Yot-

   c. Drap-

   d. Rabi-

12. Choose the stem word that means not tense.

   a. Hommi-

   b. Lax-

   c. –Tic

   d. Tens-

13. Choose the stem word that means mental illness.

   a. Kilm-

   b. Cher-

   c. Mania-

   d. Logy-

14. Choose the stem word that means greater.

   a. Cede-

   b. Culp-

   c. Maj-

   d. Lar-

15. Choose the stem word that means light.

    a. Lumin-

    b. Radi-

    c. Scope-

    d. Promu-

16. Choose the stem word that means eight.

    a. Kine-

    b. Zeb-

    c. Oct-

    d. Puin-

17. Choose the stem word that means movement, motion.

    a. Kis-

    b. Kine-

    c. Trid-

    d. Agog-

18. Choose the stem word that means child.

    a. Dropi-

    b. Calp-

    c. Ped-

    d. Small-

19. Choose the stem word that means fifth.

    a. Quint-

    b. Ward-

    c. Caldi-

    d. Scor-

Vocabulary - Unlocking Big Ideas

20. Choose the stem word that means empty.

    a. Odor-

    b. Vac-

    c. Mar-

    d. Nema-

21. Choose the stem word that means animal, living being.

    a. Ery-

    b. Brat(o)-

    c. Anis-

    d. Zo-

22. Choose the stem word that means before.

    a. Hered-

    b. Pre-

    c. Part-

    d. Jug-

23. Choose the stem word that means end.

    a. Grou-

    b. Stari-

    c. Fin-

    d. Ladi-

24. Choose the stem word that means word.

    a. Nauti-

    b. Baro-

    c. Justi-

    d. Verb-

25. Choose the stem word that means sphere.

    a. Curv-

    b. Glob-

    c. Blob-

    d. Derog-

Vocabulary- Unlocking Big Ideas

Answer Key Part II

1. C
The stem root word aero- means air, atmosphere, for example, aeronautics and aerosol.

2. D
The stem root word femin- means relating to women, female, for example femininity.

3. B
The stem root word fin-means end, for example finish and final.

4. A
The stem root word bi(o)- means life, for example, biology, biologist and biosphere.

5. D
The stem root word extrem- means outermost, utmost, for example extremity.

6. C
The stem root word basi- means at the bottom, for example basic and basis.

7. A
The stem root word hospit- means host, for example hospitality.

8. D
The stem root word ethn- means people, race, tribe, nation, for example ethnic and ethnicity.

9. C
The stem root word ide(o)- means idea or thought, for example ideogram and ideology.

10. C
The stem root word inter- means among or between, for ex-

ample intercollegiate, intermission and intersection.

11. A
The stem root word juven- means young or youth, for example juvenile, rejuvenate.

12. B
The stem root word lax- means not tense, for example laxative and relaxation.

13. C
The stem root word mania- means relating to mental illness, for example kleptomania and maniac.

14. C
The stem root word maj- means greater, for example majesty, majority.

15. A
The stem root word lumin- means light, for example illumination and luminous.

16. C
The stem root word oct- means eight, for example octagon and octahedron.

17. B
The stem root word kine- means air movement, motion, for example telekinesis, kinetic energy and kinesthetic.

18. C
The stem root word ped- means child, for example pedagogy.

19. A
The stem root word quint- means fifth, for example quinary and quintet.

20. B
The stem root word vac- means empty, for example vacancy, vacation and vacuum.

21. D
The stem root word zo- means animal, living being, for example, protozoa, zoo and zoology.

VOCABULARY- UNLOCKING BIG IDEAS

22. B

The stem root word pre- means before, for example previous.

23. C

The stem root word fin- means relating to end, for example finish and final.

24. D

The stem root word verb- means relating to word, for example verbal, verbatim, verbosity.

25. B

The stem root word glob- means relating to sphere, for example global and globule.

Most Common Prefix

A prefix is a word part at the beginning of a word which helps create the meaning. Understanding prefix is a powerful tool for increasing your vocabulary because many prefix are used by two, three or more words. The word prefix contains a prefix "pre-," which means before. If you know the meaning of the prefix, you can guess the meaning of the word, even if you are not familiar with the word.

Prefix may have more than one meaning. Here is a list of 100 commonly used prefixes along with their meaning and an example of their use.

Study the list below and then answer the questions below.

Prefix	Meaning	Example
a-, am-	without	Amoral, amateur
acro-	high up	acropolis, acrobat
ab-	away	abduction, abstain
anti-	against	antidote, antivirus, antifreeze
com-, con-	together	conference, confer
con-tra-, contro	against, opposite	contradiction, contraception
crypto-	hidden	cryptography
demo-	people, nation	demographics
extra-	more than	extracurricular, extramural
hyper-	over, more	hyperactive
homo-	same	homonym, homosexual
im-, ir-, il-, in-	not, without	illegal, inconsiderate,
inter-	between	Intersect, interstate
intra	within	intramural, intranet
intro-	in, into	Introspect, introduction
multi-	many	multimillionaire, multiple
mis-	bad, wrong	miscarriage
micro-	small, million	microscope, microgram
micro-	one millionth	microgram, microeconomics

Vocabulary- Unlocking Big Ideas

mal-, mis	bad	maladjusted, malware, mistake
mini-	small	miniskirt, miniscule
multi	many	multiple, multiplicity
non-	not, without	Nonentity, nonconformist
omni-	all, every	omniscient, omnivore
octa	eight	octagon, octopus
pre-	before	preview, precedent
penta-	five	pentagon
pro-	in favor of	pro-choice, promotion
poly-	many	polygon, polyglot
quadr-, quart-	four	quadrangle, quadruple
retro-	backward	retrospect, retro
sub-	under	submarine, subterranean
semi-	half	semi-automatic , semi-
super-	extremely	superhuman, supernatural
tele-	long distance	Telephoto, telecommunication
thermo	heat	thermos
tri-	three	triangle, tricolor
thermo	heat	thermometer
un-	not, opposite	unconstitutional
uni-	one, single	unification
ultra	beyond	ultraviolet
zoo-	relating to animals	zoology

Prefix Answer Sheet

	A	B	C	D	E		A	B	C	D	E
1	○	○	○	○	○	21	○	○	○	○	○
2	○	○	○	○	○	22	○	○	○	○	○
3	○	○	○	○	○	23	○	○	○	○	○
4	○	○	○	○	○	24	○	○	○	○	○
5	○	○	○	○	○	25	○	○	○	○	○
6	○	○	○	○	○						
7	○	○	○	○	○						
8	○	○	○	○	○						
9	○	○	○	○	○						
10	○	○	○	○	○						
11	○	○	○	○	○						
12	○	○	○	○	○						
13	○	○	○	○	○						
14	○	○	○	○	○						
15	○	○	○	○	○						
16	○	○	○	○	○						
17	○	○	○	○	○						
18	○	○	○	○	○						
19	○	○	○	○	○						
20	○	○	○	○	○						

VOCABULARY- UNLOCKING BIG IDEAS
Prefix Questions

1. Choose the prefix that means single or uniform.

    a. Uni-
    b. Epic-
    c. Hydra-
    d. Si-

2. Choose the prefix that means long distance.

    a. Mini-
    b. Tele-
    c. Dis-
    d. Sci-

3. Choose the prefix that means bad.

    a. Bathy-
    b. Mal-
    c. Re-
    d. Ectos-

4. Choose the prefix that means all or every.

    a. Multi-
    b. Omni-
    c. Creo-
    d. Mal-

5. Choose the prefix that means opposite and against.

   a. Contra-
   b. Deg-
   c. Erg-
   d. Re-

6. Choose the prefix that means wrong or bad.

   a. Dis-
   b. Demo-
   c. Grad-
   d. Mis-

7. Choose the prefix that means many.

   a. Poly-
   b. Pro-
   c. Pan-
   d. Recti-

8. Choose the prefix that means before.

   a. Anti
   b. Tachy-
   c. Pre-
   d. Quin-

9. Choose the best meaning of the prefix anti.

   a. Water
   b. Enemies
   c. Against
   d. Missing the mark

VOCABULARY- UNLOCKING BIG IDEAS

10. Choose the best meaning of the prefix thermo.

   a. Long distance
   b. Heat
   c. Hard
   d. Pressure

11. Choose the best meaning of the prefix intra.

   a. Square shape
   b. Between
   c. Round
   d. Border line

12. Choose the best meaning of the prefix multi.

   a. Blood
   b. Severe pain
   c. Narrow
   d. Many

13. Choose the best meaning of the prefix mini.

   a. Harsh
   b. Acute
   c. Small
   d. Larger than normal

14. Choose the best meaning of the prefix octa.

   a. Extreme
   b. Eight
   c. Short
   d. Water animal

15. Choose the best meaning of the prefix pro.

   a. Extremely cold
   b. Before
   c. In favor of
   d. Repeat

16. Choose the best meaning of the prefix quad.

   a. 3-Sided
   b. Four
   c. Five
   d. Many sided

17. Choose the best meaning of the prefix retro.

   a. Related to temperature
   b. Against
   c. Deny
   d. Backward

18. Choose the best meaning of the prefix semi.

   a. Half
   b. Complete
   c. Related to money
   d. Related to weapons

19. Choose the best meaning of the prefix ultra.

   a. Double
   b. Far beyond
   c. Slow
   d. Related to health

VOCABULARY- UNLOCKING BIG IDEAS

20. Choose the best meaning of the prefix tri.

    a. Three

    b. Acrobat

    c. Related to time

    d. Related to air

21. Choose the best meaning of the prefix un.

    a. Alone

    b. Together

    c. Opposite

    d. Agreement

22. Choose the best meaning of the prefix zoo.

    a. Same time

    b. Relating to animals

    c. Related to the forest

    d. Large house

23. Choose the best meaning of the prefix homo.

    a. Same

    b. Red in color

    c. Related to blood

    d. Hard

24. Choose the best meaning of the prefix super.

    a. Extremely

    b. Relating to animals

    c. Related to the forest

    d. Large house

25. Choose the best meaning of the prefix intro.

    a. Same

    b. Red in color

    c. Into

    d. Hard

VOCABULARY- UNLOCKING BIG IDEAS

Answer Key

1. A
The prefix uni means single and uniform, for example unification.

2. B
The prefix tele means long distance, for example telecommunication.

3. B
The prefix mal means bad, for example maladjusted.

4. B
The prefix omni means all or every, for example omniscient.

5. A
The prefix contra means opposite or against, for example contradiction.

6. D
The prefix mis means wrong or bad, for example misstep or miscarriage.

7. A
The prefix poly means many, for example polygon.

8. C
The prefix pre means before, for example preview.

9. C
The prefix anti means against, for example, antichrist.

10. B
The prefix thermo means heat, for example thermostat.

11. B
The prefix intra means between, for example intravenous.

12. D
The prefix multi means many, for example multiple.

13. C
The prefix mini means small, for example miniscule.

14. B
The prefix octa means eight, for example octagon.

15. C
The prefix pro means in favor of, for example promotion.

16. B
The prefix quad means four, for example quadruped, or four legs.

17. D
The prefix retro means backward, for example retrospect.

18. A
The prefix semi means half, for example semi-detached.

19. B
The prefix ultra means far beyond, for example ultraviolet.

20. A
The prefix tri means three, for example trilogy.

21. C
The prefix un means opposite and not, for example unconstitutional.

22. B
The prefix zoo means animal, for example zoology.

23. A
The prefix homo means same, for example homosexual.

24. A
The prefix super means extreme, for example supernatural.

25. C
The prefix intro means into, for example introspect.

Vocabulary- Unlocking Big Ideas
Most Common Synonyms

Synonyms, like prefix and stem words are a great two-for-one strategy for improving your vocabulary fast. Below is a list of the most common synonyms followed by 30 questions.

Word	Synonym	Synonym
Amazing	Extraordinary	Astonishing
Aggravate	Infuriate	Annoy
Arrogant	Imperious	Disdainful
Answer	Respond	Reply
Antagonist	Enemy	Adversary
Attain	Achieve	Reach
Benevolence	Kindness	Charitable
Berate	Disapprove	Criticize
Beautiful	Gorgeous	Attractive
Big	Gigantic	Enormous
Boisterous	Loud	Rowdy
Boring	Uninteresting	Dull
Budget	Plan	Allot
Contradict	Oppose	Deny
Category	Division	Classification
Complete	Comprehensive	Total
Conspicuous	Prominent	Bold
Catch	Seize	Capture
Chubby	Fat	Plump
Congenial	Pleasant	Friendly
Criticize	Berate	Belittle
Delicious	Delectable	Appetizing
Describe	Portray	Picture
Destroy	Ruin	Wreck
Dwindle	Diminish	Abate
Difference	Contrast	Dissimilarity
Decay	Rot	Decompose
Decent	Pure	Honorable
Decipher	Decode	Decrypt
Eager	Enthusiastic	Willing
Word	**Synonym**	**Synonym**

Elaborate	Enhance	Explain
Explain	Elaborate	Elucidate
Eccentric	Weird	Odd
Embezzle	Misappropriate	Steal
Fastidious	Exacting	Particular
Flatter	Praise	Compliment
Fantasy	Imagine	Day dream
Fondle	Caress	Stroke
Furious	Raging	Angry
Good	Sound	Excellent
Genuine	Real	Actual
Gay	Happy	Cheerful
Ghastly	Horrible	Gruesome
Handicap	Disadvantage	Disability
Haughty	Proud	Arrogant
Hypocrisy	Pretense	Duplicity
Humiliate	Shame	Humble
Interesting	Captivating	Engaging
Illicit	Illegal	Unlawful
Immaterial	Irrelevant	Unimportant
Illustrious	Famous	Noble
Impregnable	Unconquerable	Unbeatable
Incoherent	Jumbled	Confused
Dishonest	Deceitful	Duplicitous
Itinerary	Schedule	Route
Intrusive	Invasive	Nosy
Jargon	Slang	Lingo
Jovial	Jolly	Genial
Juvenile	Immature	Adolescent
Justification	Reason	Excuse
Jostle	Shove	Push
Keep	Hold	Retain
Keen	Sharp	Acute
Keel	Swagger	Reel
Look	Gaze	Inspect
Little	Tiny	Small

Vocabulary - Unlocking Big Ideas

Word	Synonym	Synonym
Limitation	Constraint	Boundary
Least	Lowest	Minimum
Malice	Bitterness	Spite
Match	Identical	Correspond
Memorial	Commemorate	Monument
Meager	Bare	Scanty
Memento	Gift	Keepsake
Necessary	Required	Essential
Negotiate	Scheme	Bargain
Novice	Learner	Beginner
Narrate	Disclose	Tell
Negligible	Unimportant	Insignificant
Obstinate	Adamant	Stubborn
Omen	Premonition	Foreboding
Opulence	Abundance	Wealth
Omit	Exclude	Disregard
Perplex	Confuse	Astonish
Parcel	Bundle	Package
Pause	Wait	Break
Plight	Situation	Scenario
Quack	Fake	Charlatan
Quip	Joke	Jest
Renown	Famous	Popular
Radiate	Emanate	Effuse
Run	Accelerate	Dash
Romantic	Amorous	Loving
Rebel	Dissent	Renegade
Reconcile	Harmonize	Conciliate
Render	Give	Present
Sanction	Authorize	Approve
Satisfy	Sate	Gratify
Strong	Powerful	Hard
Sealed	Stroll	Walk
Shackle	Retrain	Confine
Saunter	Shut	Close
Terminate	End	Finish
True	Accurate	Factual
Thrive	Prosper	Progress

Word	Synonym	Synonym
Tumult	Confusion	Disturbance
Tacit	Implicit	Implied
Terminate	End	Finish
Thaw	Unfreeze	Defrost
Update	Modernize	Renew
Ultimate	Supreme	Eventual
Uncanny	Mysterious	Spooky
Valid	Accurate	Legitimate
Verify	Validate	Certify
Vacate	Quit	Resign
Various	Assortment	Diverse
Wrath	Rage	Fury
Weird	Strange	Odd
Yearly	Annually	Year by year
Yank	Pull	Draw
Yearn	Long for	Desire
Zealous	Enthusiastic	Dedicated
Zoom	Speed off	Hurry

Vocabulary – Unlocking Big Ideas
Synonym Practice

Synonym Practice Questions

1. Select the synonym of conspicuous.

    a. Important

    b. Prominent

    c. Beautiful

    d. Convincing

2. Select the synonym of benevolence.

    a. Happiness

    b. Courage

    c. Kindness

    d. Loyalty

3. Select the synonym of boisterous.

    a. Loud

    b. Soft

    c. Gentle

    d. Warm

4. Select the synonym of fondle.

    a. Hold

    b. Caress

    c. Throw

    d. Keep

VOCABULARY- UNLOCKING BIG IDEAS

5. Select the synonym of impregnable.

    a. Unconquerable

    b. Impossible

    c. Unlimited

    d. Imperfect

6. Select the synonym of antagonist.

    a. Supporter

    b. Fan

    c. Enemy

    d. Partner

7. Select the synonym of memento.

    a. Monument

    b. Remembrance

    c. Gift

    d. Idea

8. Select the synonym of insidious.

    a. Wise

    b. Brave

    c. Helpful

    d. Deceitful

9. Select the synonym of itinerary.

    a. Schedule

    b. Guidebook

    c. Pass

    d. Diary

10. Select the synonym of illustrious.

   a. Rich

   b. Noble

   c. Gallant

   d. Poor

11. Select the pair below that are synonyms.

   a. Jargon and Slang

   b. Slander and Plagiarism

   c. Devotion and Devout

   d. Current and Outdated

12. Select the pair below that are synonyms.

   a. Render and Give

   b. Recognition and Cognizant

   c. Stem and Root

   d. Adjust and Redo

13. Select the pair below that are synonyms.

   a. Private and Public

   b. Intrusive and Invasive

   c. Mysterious and Unknown

   d. Common and Unique

14. Select the pair below that are synonyms.

   a. Renowned and Popular

   b. Guard and Safe

   c. Aggressive and Shy

   d. Curtail and Avoid

VOCABULARY- UNLOCKING BIG IDEAS

15. Select the pair below that are synonyms.

   a. Brevity and Ambiguous

   b. Fury and Light-hearted

   c. Incoherent and Jumbled

   d. Benign And Malignant

16. Select the pair below that are synonyms.

   a. Congenial and Pleasant

   b. Distort and Similar

   c. Valuable and Rich

   d. Asset and Liability

17. Select the pair below that are synonyms.

   a. Circumstance and Plan

   b. Negotiate and Scheme

   c. Ardent and Whimsical

   d. Plight and Situation

18. Select the pair below that are synonyms.

   a. Berate and Criticize

   b. Unspoken and Unknown

   c. Tenet and Favor

   d. Turf and Seashore

19. Select the pair below that are synonyms.

   a. Adequate and Inadequate

   b. Sate and Satisfy

   c. Sufficient and Lacking

   d. Spectator and Teacher

20. Select the pair below that are synonyms.

    a. Pensive and Alibi

    b. Terminate and End

    c. Plot and Point

    d. Jaded and Honest

CHOOSE THE SYNONYM OF THE UNDERLINED WORD

21. I cannot wait to try some of the <u>delectable</u> dishes served in the new restaurant.

    a. Unique

    b. Expensive

    c. New

    d. Delicious

22. Can you <u>describe</u> the character of Juliet in the play?

    a. Report

    b. Portray

    c. State

    d. Draw

23. The soldiers <u>destroyed</u> the rebel's camp.

    a. Ruined

    b. Ended

    c. Fixed

    d. Conquered

Vocabulary- Unlocking Big Ideas

24. There is a big <u>difference</u> in Esther Pete's grades.

    a. Complication

    b. Dissimilarity

    c. Minus

    d. Increase

25. I can <u>attain</u> my goals in life when I study hard.

    a. Finish

    b. Forget

    c. Effect

    d. Achieve

26. The lecture was so <u>boring</u> everybody was starting to get sleepy.

    a. Uninteresting

    b. Sensible

    c. Fast

    d. Exciting

27. The <u>eager</u> crowd yelled and cheered for their favorite team during the basketball tournament.

    a. Bored

    b. Uninterested

    c. Angry

    d. Enthusiastic

28. The government is planning to <u>end</u> famine through mass food production.

    a. Close

    b. Avoid

    c. Stop

    d. Start

29. Children <u>enjoy</u> playing in the park with their playmates.

    a. Dislike

    b. Relish

    c. Spend

    d. Uninterested

30. Can you <u>elaborate</u> on the reason behind your tardiness?

    a. Define

    b. Correct

    c. Explain

    d. Interpret

Vocabulary- Unlocking Big Ideas
Synonym Practice Answer Key

1. B
Conspicuous and prominent are synonyms.

2. C
Benevolence and kindness are synonyms.

3. A
Boisterous and loud are synonyms.

4. B
Fondle and caress are synonyms.

5. A
Impregnable and unconquerable are synonyms.

6. C
Antagonist and enemy are synonyms.

7. C
Memento and gift are synonyms.

8. D
Insidious and deceitful are synonyms.

9. A
Itinerary and schedule are synonyms.

10. B
Illustrious and noble are synonyms.

11. A
Jargon and slang are synonyms.

12. A
Render and give are synonyms.

13. B
Intrusive and invasive are synonyms.

14. A
Renowned and popular are synonyms.

15. C
Incoherent and jumbled are synonyms.

16. A
Congenial and pleasant are synonyms.

17. D
Plight and situation are synonyms.

18. A
Berate and criticize are synonyms.

19. B
Sate and satisfy are synonyms.

20. B
Terminate and end are synonyms.

21. D
Delectable and delicious are synonyms.

22. B
Describe and portray are synonyms.

23. A
Destroy and ruin are synonyms.

24. B
Difference and dissimilarity are synonyms.

25. D
Attain and achieve are synonyms.

26. A
Boring and uninteresting are synonyms.

27. D
Eager and enthusiastic are synonyms.

28. C
End and stop are synonyms.

29. B
Enjoy and relish are synonyms.

30. C
Elaborate and explain are synonyms.

Most Common Antonyms

Antonyms, like synonyms and stems, are a great two-for-one strategy for increasing your vocabulary. Below is a list of the most common antonyms, following by practice questions.

Word	Antonym	Antonym
Abundant	Scarce	Insufficient
Abnormal	Standard	Normal
Advance	Retreat	Recoil
Aimless	Directed	Motivated
Absurd	Sensible	Wise
Authentic	Imitation	Fake
Benevolence	Animosity	Indifference
Bloodless	Sensitive	Feeling
Blissful	Miserable	Sorrowful
Brilliant	Dulled	Dark
Certainty	Uncertainty	Doubtful
Capable	Inept	Incompetent
Cease	Begin	Commence
Charge	Discharge	Exonerate
Cohesive	Weak	Yielding
Console	Aggravate	Annoy
Confused	Enlightened	Attentive
Captivity	Liberty	Freedom
Diligent	Negligent	Languid
Dreadful	Pleasant	Pleasing
Decisive	Procrastinating	Indecisive
Deranged	Sane	Sensible
Disable	Enable	Assist
Discord	Harmony	Cooperation
Disjointed	Connected	Attached
Dogmatic	Flexible	Amenable
Erratic	Consistent	Dependable
Ecstatic	Despaired	Tormented
Eligible	Improper	Unfit
Escalate	Diminish	Decrease

VOCABULARY- UNLOCKING BIG IDEAS

Word	Antonym	Antonym
Elusive	Confronting	Attracting
Exhibit	Conceal	Hide
Fidelity	Disloyalty	Infidelity
Factual	Imprecise	Incorrect
Fearful	Courageous	Brave
Famous	Obscure	Unknown
Gaunt	Plump	Thick
Graceful	Awkward	Careless
Goodness	Meanness	Wickedness
Glamorous	Irritating	Offensive
Hard	Soft	Pliable
Hoarse	Smooth	Pleasing
Hidden	Bare	Exposed
Hearty	Apathetic	Lethargic
Harmful	Harmless	Safe
Harsh	Mild	Gentle
Idiotic	Smart	Intelligent
Idle	Busy	Working
Illegal	Lawful	Authorized
Illicit	Legal	Lawful
Illuminate	Obfuscate	Confuse
Immense	Tiny	Small
Intimate	Formal	Unfriendly
Identical	Opposite	Different
Immense	Minute	Tiny
Justice	Lawlessness	Unfairness
Jealous	Content	Trusting
Joyful	Sorrowful	Sad
Jumpy	Composed	Collected
Knack	Inability	Ineptitude
Kill	Create	Bear
Keen	Uninterested	Reluctant
Laughable	Serious	Grave
Latter	Former	First
Legible	Unreadable	Unclear
Literal	Figurative	Metaphorical
Loathe	Love	Like
Legendary	Factual	True

Word	Antonym	Antonym
Large	Little	Small
Miserable	Cheerful	Joyful
Moderate	Excessive	Unrestrained
Magical	Boring	Ordinary
Minor	Major	Significant
Myriad	Few	Scant
Narrow	Broad	Wide
Nasty	Pleasant	Magnificent
Nimble	Awkward	Clumsy
Optional	Compulsory	Required
Operational	Inactive	Inoperative
Optimistic	Pessimistic	Doubtful
Ordinary	Abnormal	Uncommon
Pester	Delight	Please
Penalize	Forgive	Reward
Placate	Agitate	Upset
Practical	Unfeasible	Unrealistic
Pensive	Shallow	Ignorant
Queasy	Comfortable	Satisfied
Quietly	Loudly	Audibly
Quirky	Conventional	Normal
Qualified	Unqualified	Incapable
Rapid	Slow	Leisurely
Refuse	Agree	Assent
Reluctant	Enthusiastic	Excited
Romantic	Realistic	Pragmatic
Ridicule	Flatter	Praise
Refresh	Damage	Ruin
Rough	Level	Smooth
Sacrifice	Refuse	Hold
Sadistic	Humane	Kind
Sane	Deranged	Insane
Save	Spend	Splurge
Scarce	Abundant	Plenty
Scorn	Approve	Delight
Scatter	Gather	Collect
Shrink	Expand	Grow
Simple	Complex	Complicated

VOCABULARY- UNLOCKING BIG IDEAS

Word	Antonym	Antonym
Stingy	Generous	Bountiful
Sterile	Dirty	Infected
Tedious	Interesting	Exciting
Tactful	Indiscreet	Careless
Tough	Weak	Vulnerable
Transparent	Opaque	Cloudy
Terminate	Initiate	Start
Truth	Lie	Untruth
Understand	Misunderstand	Misinterpret
Usable	Useless	Unfit
Validate	Veto	Reject
Vanquish	Endorse	Surrender
Vanish	Appear	Materialize
Vicious	Gentle	Nice
Vice	Virtue	Propriety
Villain	Hero	Savior
Vulnerable	Strong	Powerful
Wary	Reckless	Careless
Wasteful	Frugal	Thrifty
Wane	Grow	Increase
Weary	Lively	Energetic
Young	Old	Mature
Yonder	Nearby	Close
Zealous	Lethargic	Unenthusiastic

Antonym Practice Answer Sheet

	A	B	C	D	E			A	B	C	D	E
1	○	○	○	○	○		21	○	○	○	○	○
2	○	○	○	○	○		22	○	○	○	○	○
3	○	○	○	○	○		23	○	○	○	○	○
4	○	○	○	○	○		24	○	○	○	○	○
5	○	○	○	○	○		25	○	○	○	○	○
6	○	○	○	○	○		26	○	○	○	○	○
7	○	○	○	○	○		27	○	○	○	○	○
8	○	○	○	○	○		28	○	○	○	○	○
9	○	○	○	○	○		29	○	○	○	○	○
10	○	○	○	○	○		30	○	○	○	○	○
11	○	○	○	○	○							
12	○	○	○	○	○							
13	○	○	○	○	○							
14	○	○	○	○	○							
15	○	○	○	○	○							
16	○	○	○	○	○							
17	○	○	○	○	○							
18	○	○	○	○	○							
19	○	○	○	○	○							
20	○	○	○	○	○							

Vocabulary- Unlocking Big Ideas
Antonym Practice Questions

1. Choose the antonym pair.

    a. Abundant and Scarce

    b. Several and Plenty

    c. Analysis and Review

    d. Obtrusive and Hierarchical

2. Choose the antonym pair.

    a. Bully and Animal

    b. Teary-eyed and Gentle

    c. Tough and Weak

    d. Strong and Massive

3. Choose the antonym pair.

    a. Illuminate and Obfuscate

    b. Resonance and Significance

    c. Resonate and Justify

    d. Rationalize and Practice

4. Choose the antonym pair.

    a. Simple and Complex

    b. Plain and Plaid

    c. Shy and Sinister

    d. Vibrant and Cheery

5. Choose the antonym pair.

   a. Elevate and Escalate

   b. Exhibit and Conceal

   c. Boast and Brood

   d. Show and Contest

6. Choose the antonym pair.

   a. Strict and Tight

   b. Hurtful and Offensive

   c. Unpleasant and Mean

   d. Stingy and Generous

7. Choose the antonym pair.

   a. New and Torn

   b. Advance and Retreat

   c. Next and Last

   d. Followed and Continued

8. Choose the antonym pair.

   a. Halt and Speed

   b. Began and Amidst

   c. Stop and Delay

   d. Cease and Begin

9. Choose the antonym pair.

   a. Scary and Horrific

   b. Honor and Justice

   c. Immense and Tiny

   d. Vague and Loud

VOCABULARY- UNLOCKING BIG IDEAS

10. Choose the antonym pair.

   a. Dissatisfied and Unsatisfied

   b. Disentangle and Acknowledge

   c. Discord and Harmony

   d. Fruition and Fusion

11. Choose the antonym pair.

   a. Late and Later

   b. Latter and Former

   c. Structure and Organization

   d. Latter and Rushed

12. Choose the antonym pair.

   a. Belittle and Bemuse

   b. Shrunk and Minimal

   c. Shrink and Expand

   d. Smelly and Odor

13. Choose the antonym pair.

   a. Repulsive and Repentant

   b. Reluctant and Enthusiastic

   c. Prepare and Ready

   d. Release and Give

14. Choose the antonym pair.

   a. Sovereign and Autonomy

   b. Disdain and Contempt

   c. Disorder and Disarray

   d. Refuse and Agree

15. Choose the antonym pair.

    a. Gentle and Soft

    b. Fragile and Breakable

    c. Vulnerable and Strong

    d. Vain and Tidy

16. Select the antonym of authentic.

    a. Real

    b. Imitation

    c. Apparition

    d. Dream

17. Select the antonym of villain.

    a. Actor

    b. Actress

    c. Heroine

    d. Hero

18. Select the antonym of vanish.

    a. Appear

    b. Lose

    c. Reflection

    d. Empty

19. Select the antonym of literal.

    a. Manuscript

    b. Writing

    c. Figurative

    d. Untrue

Vocabulary- Unlocking Big Ideas

20. Select the antonym of harsh.

    a. Mild

    b. Light

    c. Bulky

    d. Bothersome

21. Select the antonym of splurge.

    a. Spend

    b. Count

    c. Use

    d. Save

22. Select the antonym of idle.

    a. Occupied

    b. Vacant

    c. Busy

    d. Interested

23. Select the antonym of console.

    a. Aggravate

    b. Empathize

    c. Sympathize

    d. Cry

24. Select the antonym of deranged.

    a. Chaos

    b. Dirty

    c. Bleak

    d. Sane

25. Select the antonym of disjointed.

   a. Connected
   b. Dismayed
   c. Recognized
   d. Bountiful

26. Select the antonym of confused.

   a. Frustrated
   b. Ashamed
   c. Enlightened
   d. Unknown

27. Select the antonym of benevolent.

   a. Nice
   b. Mature
   c. Honest
   d. Indifferent

28. Select the antonym of illicit.

   a. Unlawful
   b. Legal
   c. Anonymous
   d. Deceitful

29. Select the antonym of sterile.

   a. Dirty
   b. Alcoholic
   c. Drunk

VOCABULARY - CRACKING THE CODE

d. Drug

30. Select the antonym of myriad.

a. Many

b. Several

c. Few

d. Plenty

Antonyms Answer Key

1. A
Abundant and scarce are antonyms.

2. C
Tough and weak are antonyms.

3. A
Illuminate and obfuscate are antonyms.

4. A
Simple and complex are antonyms.

5. B
Exhibit and conceal are antonyms.

6. D
Stingy and generous are antonyms.

7. B
Advance and retreat are antonyms.

8. D
Cease and begin are antonyms.

9. C
Immense and tiny are antonyms.

10. C
Discord and harmony are antonyms.

11. B
Latter and former are antonyms.

12. C
Shrink and expand are antonyms.

13. B
Reluctant and enthusiastic are antonyms.

14. D
Refuse and agree are antonyms.

15. C
Vulnerable and strong are antonyms.

16. B
Authentic and imitation are antonyms.

17. D
Villain and hero are antonyms.

18. A
Vanish and appear are antonyms.

19. C
Literal and figurative are antonyms.

20. A
Harsh and mild are antonyms.

21. D
Splurge and save are antonyms.

22. C
Idle and busy are antonyms.

23. A
Console and aggravate are antonyms.

24. D
Deranged and sane are antonyms.

25. A
Disjointed and connected are antonyms.

26. C
Confused and enlightened are antonyms.

27. D
Benevolent and indifferent are antonyms.

28. B
Illicit and legal are antonyms.

29. A
Sterile and dirty are antonyms.

30. C
Myriad and few are antonyms.

Your Game Day Strategy: Calm, Cool, and Collected

The "Morning Of" Routine

Think of today like a marathon. You wouldn't start a race without shoes, and you shouldn't start this test without a solid foundation.

- **Fuel the Engine:** Eat a breakfast that sticks to your ribs. Porridge, eggs, or toast—something steady. Avoid the "Big Prep" mistake of loading up on too much caffeine; you want focused energy, not the jitters.
- **The "Double-Check" Bag:** Before you leave the house, make sure you have your ID, your registration info, and those sharpened pencils. Don't leave this for the last minute—scrambling for a lost ID is a recipe for instant stress.
- **Leave Early:** In Victoria, we know traffic or the bus can be unpredictable. Give yourself an extra 20 minutes. Arriving early lets you sit in your car or on a bench and just *breathe* for a moment before heading in.

- **The "No-Study" Zone:** Once you leave the house, put the books away. Trying to cram one last root word into your brain while walking through the door only creates panic. Trust that the work you've done over the last three weeks is already in there.

Wrestling the "Test Anxiety" Monster

If you're sitting at that desk and feel your heart start to race, try these three simple tricks I've taught my students over the years:

1. The "Box Breath" If you feel overwhelmed, stop for 10 seconds. Inhale for 4 counts, hold for 4, exhale for 4, and hold for 4. It signals to your brain that there's no "real" danger. It's a reset button for your nervous system.
2. The "Five-Minute Wall" Sometimes the first page looks like Greek. If you hit a wall, don't panic. Skip the first two questions and find one you *know* you can answer. Getting one "win" under your belt breaks the spell of anxiety and gets your momentum back.
3. Change Your Perspective Instead of thinking, *"I have to pass this or else,"* try thinking, *"I've practiced for this, and I'm just here to show what I know."* You aren't being judged as a person; you're just solving some puzzles on a piece of paper.

Prep companies love to make these tests sound like life-or-death situations. They aren't. They are just a hurdle on a track you've already been running. You've jumped higher hurdles than this in your life, I'm sure of it.

During the Exam

- **Eyes on Your Own Paper:** Don't worry about how fast the person next to you is flipping pages. They aren't you. Some people rush and make mistakes; you are going for accuracy.
- **The "Weeding" Method:** On tough vocabulary or math questions, focus on crossing out the "crazy" answers first. Even if you don't know the right one, narrowing it down to two choices makes it much less scary.

- **Take Micro-Breaks:** Every 15 minutes, put your pencil down, roll your shoulders, stretch your fingers, and take one deep breath. It takes five seconds, but it keeps the "test fog" from setting in.

You've got the knowledge, you've got the plan, and now you've got the mindset. Take a deep breath—you're ready for this.

The Starting Line: Your Journey Begins Here

You did it. If you're reading this page, it means you've put in the hours, wrestled with the math, and sharpened your vocabulary. You didn't take the easy way out, and that speaks volumes about the kind of student—and professional—you're going to be.

In my years of teaching and publishing here in Victoria, I've seen a lot of students sit at their kitchen tables just like you're doing now. The ones who succeed aren't always the "natural test-takers"; they're the ones who show up, do the work, and refuse to be intimidated by a timer or a tricky word problem.

Getting into your program is a massive milestone. It's the door that opens up to a career that will challenge you, reward you, and change your life. You've given yourself the best possible tool for that journey: preparation.

A Final Bit of Advice
As you head toward your exam date, remember to:

Trust your prep: You've done the practice tests. You know the material.

Keep your head up: If you hit a tough question, don't let it rattle you. Just move to the next one and come back if you have time.

Take care of the human element: Get a good night's sleep, eat a solid breakfast, and remember that you are more than just a test score.

We're rooting for you. At the end of the day, our mission is to make sure the "forgotten" student—the one working a job while studying late at night—has exactly what they need to thrive. You've got this.

Study. Practice. Succeed.

Let's Stay in Touch

Things change—tests get updated, and new tips come across my desk all the time. I'd love to keep supporting you as you get ready.

Register for Free Updates & More Practice Questions Head over to https://test-preparation.ca/register/ to register your book. You'll get the latest test tips, updates, and even more practice questions sent straight to you.

Online Resources

How to Prepare for a Test - The Ultimate Guide

https://www.test-preparation.ca/prepare-test/

Learning Styles - The Complete Guide

https://www.test-preparation.ca/learning-style/

Test Anxiety Secrets!

https://www.test-preparation.ca/test-anxiety/

Time Management on a Test

https://www.test-preparation.ca/time-management/

Flash Cards - The Complete Guide

https://www.test-preparation.ca/flash-cards/

How to Memorize - The Complete Guide

https://www.test-preparation.ca/memorize/

Super Foods for Studying

https://test-preparation.ca/super-foods-studying/

www.ingramcontent.com/pod-product-compliance
Lightning Source LLC
Chambersburg PA
CBHW071808080526
44589CB00012B/726